IN DEFENSE

OF

FRANCE

(DÉFENSE DU PAYS)

BY

EDOUARD DALADIER

Essay Index Reprint Series

BOOKS FOR LIBRARIES PRESS

FREEPORT, NEW YORK

First Published 1939
Reprinted 1971

INTERNATIONAL STANDARD BOOK NUMBER:
0-8369-2352-9

LIBRARY OF CONGRESS CATALOG CARD NUMBER:
74-156637

PRINTED IN THE UNITED STATES OF AMERICA

TO AMERICA

W<small>HEN</small> I <small>REVISIT</small> *the district where I was born and renew my acquaintances among the peasants of my homeland, those simple men who, twenty years ago, saved France in the trenches of Verdun and the Argonne, and who, throughout the decades, have assured the greatness of our fatherland by their patient and tenacious efforts, I often hear them say:*

"How unfortunate it is not to be able to establish understanding with the whole world! At least, though, there is the consolation that there are peoples we can always understand, the Americans for example. They ask nothing but to live and to work in peace. They're like us."

Thus, in spite of the thousands of kilometers which separate us, in spite of all the differences of language, of race and of customs, the humblest people of France hold to Franco-American friendship as a certainty. For them it is founded on the fact that both French and Americans speak the language of liberty and justice.

[v]

To America

Like every other Frenchman, I am certain that France and the United States of America are two nations which ought always to be able to understand one another. They have the same ideal; they have the same desire to assure the dignity of the human being in peace and in labor.

It is, then, unnecessary to preface the translation of the principal speeches I have made during a year as Prime Minister of the Government of the Republic—since April 1938—with a series of explanations and commentaries. In spite of conditions peculiar to Europe, so different from conditions on the American continent, I hold firmly to the belief that every free citizen of the United States will know how to find beneath these words of a Frenchman the spirit of a people which wishes to base peace upon justice and to insure its life and its independence in labor and in honor.

The presentation in one volume of these speeches is only intended to enable the reader to follow, in its methodical development, the will behind the actions of my government. This will is entirely dedicated to the defense of our country, the peace of the world, and the safeguarding of liberty. Through serious difficulties, ceaselessly recurring, it has always aimed at the same goal. Tomorrow, as yesterday, it will endeavor to overcome

[vi]

To America

the dangers that threaten us and to secure with the safety of France, the safety of liberty and of the dignity of the individual.

These pages ought not, therefore, to be considered solely as a historical document relating to a period in the past. The obstacles we have already had to clear may be only the forerunners of still more serious difficulties. The action of yesterday can be of value only if it prepares and strengthens the action of tomorrow. At the moment, the writing of the history of events whose consequences are yet far from exhausted is a matter of little importance. Our fate is still in our hands and depends on our determination. What is important is to keep this determination intact and ever watchful.

I hope that these few pages will help the reader not only to get a sense of the value of yesterday's events but also to strengthen him for tomorrow's encounters.

EDOUARD DALADIER

CONTENTS

[ix]

Contents

THE URGE TO ACTION

THE GUARD ON THE FRONTIERS
OF THE EMPIRE

[x]

Contents

A PROFILE

A PROFILE

JUST OFF THE GREAT HIGHWAY which follows the valley
of the Rhône, the little city of Carpentras, once the
capital of the county of Venaissin, spreads out in the
center of a luxuriant countryside.

Few regions offer more to rejoice the eye. When the
composition of the landscape demands it, the countryside harmoniously produces a Roman ruin or a Fran-
ciscan campanile.

When the plain begins to be a little monotonous with
its olive groves, fruit trees, mulberries, broom and laven-
der, the village one hopes for arrives on schedule, bound
in by an antique rampart around which stands an alley
of enormous platanes; a village of yellow stones with a
clock-tower bonneted in wrought iron from which one
hears bells ringing.

Beyond the village, the garden of the Hesperides begins
again; apricot, peach and cherry ripen with the vine and
the olive. Beehives stand neighbors to fields of eggplants
and melons, and when a trainload of strawberries leaves

[3]

In Defense Of France

the station, it leaves a perfumed wake behind it for long miles.

Nevertheless, up to the last century, the inhabitants of this region complained of the insufficiency of the harvest gleaned from an ungrateful soil. The lack of water, the brutality of the north wind, the destructive mistral, would ruin the hopes of a year within a few hours. Twice a year torrential rains succeeding droughts carried away the best of the crops and even part of the earth itself. Sheep had difficulty in finding their subsistence in the shadow of the meager almond trees amo.1g the grasshoppers and in the clouds of dust raised by the tornado. This poor country had to be fertilized by irrigation. Under the Revolution, the reunion with France, "conformably with the oaths freely and solemnly sworn by the majority of the communes and citizens" finally permitted the region of Carpentras to progress.

And during the first half of the nineteenth century the district became covered with a network of rivulets, infinitely ramified, generators of fertility.

For centuries the family of Daladier lived in the little city of Carpentras.

[4]

A Profile

Claude Daladier, born in the middle of the last century, took part in the transformation of his natal district. Irrigation had already enriched the region where his second son, Edouard, was born in June 1884.

Grandfather Daladier was a stonemason; most of his ancestors were woodworkers. Claude had broken with this tradition, had learned to be a baker and had married a demoiselle Mouriès, the daughter of his employer.

It was thus that Edouard Daladier grew up in a baker's house, in an atmosphere always warm with the heat of the oven, among the exhilarating odors of fresh bread.

As an infant his cradlesong was the rhythmic shock of the pestle in the big wooden mixing vat, and the cadenced trembling which his heavy labors by night wring from the baker.

All day long customers kept coming and going in the bakery where Mme Daladier weighed out bread. Sacks of flour, supplies of wood arrived in heavy carts, and daily, when the baking had been finished, Claude Daladier loaded a light carriage with fresh bread, hitched up his horse and went out along the roads to deliver bread to customers in the country.

When industry is carried on at home the wife is often the soul of the household. She keeps the shop and the books, sees to it that purchases are cheaply made, as well as handling the cooking and the education of the children.

It was so in the Daladier home.

When Rose Mouriès married Claude Daladier she assumed all these duties. She carried them on all her life long without weakening. No more than her husband did she know rest or vacation. Moreover, at that time all shops kept open Sunday, batches of bread were baked that day as on the rest, and holidays produced an increase of labor because of the special cakes. Nevertheless the hard labor of Claude Daladier did not go altogether without recompense. He spent his free hours among the vines and olive trees of the estate of Lègue, a league from Carpentras. Of the five children Mme Claude Daladier had brought into the world two died young; there remained in the household two boys and a girl, but although the father envisaged for his sons no other lot than his own, the mother, preoccupied with the future, observed a difference between the older of the two boys, Gustave, and Edouard.

Yes, Gustave would make an excellent baker. He would follow his father. But Edouard, still a boy, was particularly successful in his studies. He demonstrated a taste for books, for erudition.

A Profile

After consulting his teacher in the matter, the mother sent her son to take an examination for a scholarship. He passed it at the age of ten and thereby obtained access to the imposing and austere building where they taught him Greek and Latin.

After having finished his primary classes and several years in the intermediate school at Carpentras, Edouard Daladier went to the lycée at Lyons to continue his studies. Already, like so many poor young men, scholarship students out of modest families, he envisaged a professorship at the close of his education. At Lyons he was a pupil of M. Edouard Herriot, then professor of literature and at present President of the Chamber of Deputies of France.

Examinations became frequent along the path of the young man. One after another he passed them brilliantly, with compliments and citations.

Notably, he received the diploma of Etudes Supérieurs with the citation "Very good" for having treated, to the satisfaction of the examiners, the question of the administration of a big abbey in Carolingian times, according to ancient documents.

This was, no doubt, an excellent preparation for a future minister of state.

[7]

In Defense Of France

At this time he resolved to attempt the most difficult competition of all: the Aggregation of History and Geography. He made the trip to Paris to take this examination in July 1909.

There were eighty-five candidates in the competition. Of this number fifteen were admitted; Daladier came out of the Sorbonne with the number 1.

"A very well-prepared candidate and one who has talent. Will doubtless be an excellent professor."

This was the remark of the president of the jury on candidate Edouard Daladier.

After this success Edouard Daladier returned to Carpentras, having finished his accumulation of university degrees.

In the following month of September he was nominated as professor of history and geography at the Lycée of Nîmes. His superiors there noted that he taught "with much authority and method."

But as his success at Paris gave him the right to a year's study abroad, he decided to profit by it and abandoned Nîmes after one year of teaching.

He left for Rome, for he had undertaken an important work on the Italian revolutionary movement of the nineteenth century, that which had resulted in the unity of Italy.

The pleasure of departure for the Eternal City was marred for him by an unhappy family event: the death of his mother.

It was while still wearing mourning that he installed himself at Rome, where he began long researches among the archives and libraries.

On returning to France he was appointed professor at the Lycée of Grenoble. Although it was October when he began to give his courses on French history, he was already thinking of trying politics, of presenting himself as a candidate in the forthcoming municipal election at Carpentras.

A republican, like his father and his brother, he had a profound faith in the destiny of democracy, and his studies had confirmed this faith.

Meanwhile these first political ambitions did not draw him away from his pedagogical duties, and on his return from a visit of inspection to the lycée of Grenoble, M. Gallouedec, the inspector general, gave his impressions of the young professor in the following terms:

"M. Daladier is a truly remarkable personality and one extremely interesting to study. He has qualities of the first order; his knowledge is very broad, but above all logically arranged in his mind; he has a clarity of thought which enables him to see and to throw well into relief whatever is essential or characteristic; an extraordinary manner of delivery in which accent, gestures and facial expression blend so that one cannot hear him talk without following every word he says. His voice is singularly firm and penetrating. He has an imperious authority. . . . M. Daladier is born to be the leader of a group or of a school."

M. Daladier, as one perceives, could now, according to his taste, continue in education or switch off toward politics. The judgment above, pronounced by a psychologist, left both roads open before him with the chances of success equal.

The elections were to take place in May. In January, during the New Year's vacation, Daladier had made up his platform before any of the other candidates. He had taken a sharply defined position.

Among the voters of the Left he wished to form a group of young guards opposed to the current tendency to make politics a matter of routine.

The platform of "M. Daladier, Jr" was brilliantly successful and he was elected mayor of Carpentras.

The administration of his little town, however, did not prevent the new municipal magistrate from seeking to see beyond local politics and from reflecting on the situation of France and Europe, although in 1912 very few others preoccupied themselves with such matters.

"We believe," he had occasion to say at about this time, "that the liberty of nations is a necessary condition to the progress of humanity. Our duty is that of maintaining at any price the independence of our country."

This was because "the formidable armaments of Germany" disturbed him.

Social questions did not leave him indifferent, either. He asked himself what would be the best method to follow.

"If it be true that collectivist doctrines are most often inspired by the generous desire to destroy misery and suffering, we consider that these ideas are very difficult to realize, that they suppose a sort of social miracle repugnant to reason. It would be worth more to elaborate a plan of practical reforms, conceived according to a regular method. It is chimerical to believe in a sudden social transformation, but it is necessary to continue the pursuit of abuses energetically. Safety is in action."

In Defense Of France

He expressed his faith in democracy and, in his group of friends, described himself as an "advanced republican."

M. Edouard Daladier, from that time on, returned obstinately to the foreign question. In the beginning of 1913 he said:

"Austria is preparing war against Serbia and Montenegro," and he did not believe either the denials from Vienna or those from Berlin.

"In reality," he wrote, "the victories of the Balkan peoples threw into question not only the dismemberment of Turkey, but even the existence of Austria-Hungary."

He had been inspired by reading the Viennese paper *Zeit*, then the organ of the archduke heir of Austria.

This paper maintained the following thesis: in order to maintain peace, Germany, Austria-Hungary and Italy must at all costs prevent Russia from mobilizing. In order to defeat the plans of Russia, the three allies ought to throw themselves on France and destroy her before Russia would have time to develop her own plans. The journal concluded: "A great battle won over the French, on French soil, would have the result of insuring a lasting peace."

A Profile

At Paris the Chambers were discussing the question of three years' military service, and M. Daladier noted with pleasure that in spite of differences of opinions and doctrine all parties were united on this idea, essential to the maintenance of the independence of the nation.

When the destiny of the nation was in question the country transformed itself into a whole.

A year later, M. Daladier, seated in his mayor's office at Carpentras, was preparing an appeal to the population; he had just received the telegram announcing the mobilization of the French armies.

While the alarm was ringing on all the bells of the town, of the countryside and through the entire land, people came out into the streets and formed groups in the squares. When Edouard Daladier had taken the measures necessary for keeping the city in food, for fulfilling the requisitions made by the War Department and the continuance of the vital services during his absence, he returned to his old house in the Rue de la Tour aux Eaux to pack a small suitcase and leave to join his regiment.

Both Daladier brothers were mobilized.

They bade farewell to their sister, who remained alone at home.

And, for the first time in many years—since grandfather Mouriès, since the death of Claude Daladier, the bake-oven fire was allowed to go out.

For Sergeant Daladier the war began in the neighborhood of Reims.

In September he had left the Regiment of Avignon, into which he had been mobilized, for the 2nd Regiment of the Foreign Legion, which was in need of French non-commissioned officers to handle the many foreign volunteers who had enlisted for the duration of the war.

The regiment reached the front in October.

To the fever of the first three months and the hope of a slashing campaign of a few weeks there had already succeeded a savage resolution to hold the ground.

There was no longer any question of rapid movements; "Ils, ne passeront pas" had become the watchword, the only watchword. Everyone was buried in the trenches. Rain, mud, then cold and snow followed the fine sun of the first weeks.

Daladier and his companions, simple soldiers or non-coms, fought with nature as much as with the enemy. Pick and shovel dug into the clayey soil of Champagne. The soldiers never dropped their shovels but to pick up their guns, their grenades, to spy across the parapet, kneel behind a machine gun or run, their feet heavy with mud, to the assault of enemy trenches while bullets whistled about them.

The exigencies of operations spread out the forces, called them to different sectors of the front. It was a migration of ants, concentrating around nerve centers between the sea and the Vosges.

In April 1915 Edouard Daladier's regiment was called to Artois and left the mud of Champagne for the mud of Arras. The conscripts began to learn more geography; new names, unknown yesterday, and which even his examination in history and geography had not revealed to Professor Daladier, became tragically famous in a few days: Saint Waast, Carency, Notre Dame de Lorette, Souchez.

Bearing the soft earth on their heavy shoes for four long kilometers, Daladier and his men charged through fire one day, leaving behind them fifty officers and two thousand five hundred men.

Afterward, finding itself in the rear, in bivouac, still near the front, but in dugouts against which shells did not beat, and with spring coming on, the regiment began to reorganize itself, to bind up its wounds, to eat better, smoke a peaceable pipe or two, read and write letters.

In Defense Of France

But after a new offensive near Souchez, when the muster roll was read, the battalion to which Sergeant Daladier belonged was found to be so decimated, so reduced, that it had become impossible to reconstitute it. It disappeared as a unit of attack; the survivors were distributed among the other battalions of the 2nd Regiment. And Sergeant Daladier, attached to the 209th Regiment of Infantry, went back to the east, then to Champagne, in order to participate in the September offensive in the region of Souain.

The second winter arrived.

It was not over before the French were engaged in the desperate operations of the defense of Verdun. Regiments were constantly thrown into this crucible where men were melted.

The Germans had conquered the wood of Avocourt, the hinge of the Verdun position. The French retook it, but remained there, pinned to the ground, unable to continue the advance after having reached the limits of human strength. They had to be relieved. In one of the trucks filled with the men of the 209th Infantry, rolling in the direction of the wood of Avocourt, stood the man who would one day be Minister of War of France.

The next day, when the Germans began again those

day and night attacks, furious and without respite, they encountered the men of the 209th. Fighting ceaselessly in all that tumult, under fire, fed with difficulty, and living among their dead, the men of the 209th held on for thirteen days and organized the sector.

The general commanding their division was able to write:

"The 209th, with as much method as activity, organized a position under the incessant heavy fire of the enemy and defended it against energetic attacks. The work was so well done that the position ought to be inexpugnable."

Five times the 209th Regiment had to return to the redoubt of Avocourt.

In the month of April Sergeant Daladier became an officer, and his conduct was praised in the following citation: "In the fighting in which he has taken part as a sergeant and as leader of a section, notably at Arras and the redoubt of Avocourt, has given proof of coolness, energy, and a great deal of bravery."

In Artois, the unit to which M. Daladier belonged was in touch with the English.

In the region of Châlons, where he found himself a little later, his corps was in liaison with the Russians. It was there that it was granted to Edouard Daladier to sample and to appreciate one of the last inventions of modern war—gas.

Returns to Champagne came as periodically as the seasons in the military life of Lieutenant Edouard Daladier.

When his regiment had as its objective the capture of Mont Cornillet, a high hill situated north of the mountain of Reims, which served the Germans excellently as an observation post, the assault was delivered during the night, after a long bombardment. Red rockets mounted to the heavens, bullets whistled past. The French advanced painfully through the melting snow. They moved from trench to trench, fighting hand to hand, and conquering points of resistance with grenades. Enemy groupments, taken between two fires, lifted their hands and surrendered. But the summit of the hill was organized like a fort; it was necessary to advance across open ground toward those walls of cement.

The French charged on, hiding in shell holes. Corpses marked their passage, death gave promotions, command passing from one to another like a torch.

In May Edouard Daladier was again cited in the order of the day for his conduct during the combats that lasted from April 17 to 26.

A Profile

After the long struggles in the mud, the burrowings in the trenches, the flaming attacks, returns to Verdun and Flanders; after these, citations, the cross of the Legion of Honor and promotions came to recompense Lieutenant Daladier.

M. Daladier also personally participated in the last offensives of the great war in the region of Chaulnes and La Capelle. In September he crossed the Somme, marching toward Saint Quentin. His regiment was cited in orders:

"A fine regiment which has given proof of its remarkable quality of endurance during the march to Saint Quentin. In full combat it was the first to cross the Somme and the canal; then tenaciously continued the pursuit, in spite of the losses it suffered."

Daladier finally entered Saint Quentin at the head of his soldiers. The entry into Saint Quentin took place on October 1, 1918—the First of October, an important date, the day when French children are accustomed to return to their schools!

In a year, perhaps, Lieutenant Daladier would return to his professor's chair. But if he belonged to teaching he also belonged to politics, through the mayoralty of Carpentras and through the fibers of his being. There would be elections after the war; France would be looking for new men, young men. Those who had fought in the war would have something to say with regard to the conduct of affairs in this country they had fertilized with their blood.

Several days later Lieutenant Daladier, then in the neighborhood of La Capelle, heard that German peace emissaries were being awaited.

With his policelike cap on his head, and surrounded by several officer comrades, Edouard Daladier, standing a little aside in the twilight of a melancholy autumn day, could contemplate the German plenipotentiaries who had just come through the lines and were going to ask an armistice.

Silent, stirred by the sight, the victors watched the conquered enemy advance; the enemy whose shoulders had at last been brought to touch French ground—General Von Winterfeld, Herr Erzberger and their suite.

Edouard Daladier was not yet out of his uniform when, in 1919, he became engaged to the daughter of a Paris doctor, Mlle Madeleine Laffont.

As soon as he was demobilized, he received a nomination as professor at the Lycée Condorcet in Paris. Nev-

ertheless, shortly after his marriage, he returned to his
native district with his young wife. There he began an
electoral campaign with the idea of presenting himself
in November at the legislative elections.

At Carpentras he found his brother, also demobilized,
who had once more taken over the management of the
family bakery.

The parties of the moderate Right united in 1919 to
form the Bloc National, which triumphed at the elections in a great many districts.

Nevertheless the citizens of Vaucluse voted for the
Left and M. Daladier was elected.

The Radical Socialist party, to which M. Edouard
Daladier has always belonged, is in France the party of
republican traditions. In it meet the nationalist spirit and
that of democracy. Born of the "patriots" of the French
Revolution, it has counted among its members Gam-
betta, the soul of the national defense in 1870, the deputies who in 1871 rose against a peace which would tear
Alsace and Lorraine from France, and Clemenceau.

M. Daladier thus entered the Chamber at the close of
1919 to take his seat among the members of the opposition.

In Defense Of France

In the first sessions while he was a member, Deputy Daladier merely watched and listened, quietly seated in his place. He avoided interfering in debate during the first months; he considered that his role was first that of learning, meditating and working. In this manner he sought to crystallize his opinions, to study conscientiously the problems of the hour, to settle his own mind. From the beginning he gave his particular attention to questions of foreign policy. His intellectual make-up, the earth-shaking events through which Europe had passed, the war which he had just seen from so close an observation point, led him naturally to think, on the one hand, of matters of foreign relations; on the other, of those relating to the army. His first appearance as a speaker was when he discussed the questions of Syria and Morocco; his second was in connection with the reorganization of the army. His speech was a brilliant success, and his arguments were so convincing that the Right itself applauded him. Already at this time he mentioned the thesis of the nation in arms, an idea to which he ever after remained faithful.

"The mobilization of the army ought to be that of the nation," he said again in 1923. "Our military organization thus has a double objective: that of assuring, by the formation of a healthy and well-equipped army in time of peace, the instruction of recruits and the covering of mobilization; that of creating in the several districts large military units, well staffed and having available all the resources of mobilization, prepared in advance and as carefully as the mobilization of military industry."

In the elections of 1924 the Cartel des Gauches succeeded the Bloc National with which the Right had come to power in 1919. The Radical Socialist party, which is one of the most powerful political units of the country, and which still is an important element in the alternate flux and reflux of French elections, was a heavy weight in the balance of victory.

Those familiar with parliamentary life thought at this time that M. Daladier was already designated for a ministry.

"Perhaps I will become Under-secretary of State for War, at the side of General Nollet," he himself confided to friends.

But M. Edouard Herriot, who was charged with making up a cabinet, offered him the portfolio of the Colonies. This made M. Daladier a kind of petty prime minister instead of a department head in the ministry, since the Minister of French Colonies has to consider all sorts

of matters—military, naval, aeronautical, agricultural—
and must look into the service of public health and justice as well as education, postal service and public works.

"I am busy with the improvement of the living conditions of the natives," replied the new colonial minister
when a question about his policy was put to him,
"—medical aid, instruction, protection of labor, these are
the three terms of the problem that we ought to solve.
Much has been done already. Nevertheless, not enough.
It is necessary that larger sums in the colonial budgets
be allotted to works of hygiene, instruction and the protection of workers. That is not all. I wish to orient myself
more and more toward the growing participation of all
the native elements in the administration of their countries."

He pushed forward the realization of these projects
rapidly, furnished agricultural machinery and seeds to
the natives to keep them on the soil, set on foot the
project for a railroad from the Congo to the ocean,
created the Bank of Madagascar and improved public
hygiene.

It has been said that a "Republic of Professors" succeeded to the "Republic of Lawyers," the latter having
held up to this time so important a place in the councils

of the government. It is possible to recognize at once, as far as M. Daladier is concerned, that his studies had well and solidly prepared him to play his part in affairs of state.

Among the fluctuations in public life, the reactions brought about by economic changes and financial difficulties, amid the great effervescence which followed the war, in the course of which neither France nor Europe succeeded in recovering complete equilibrium, Edouard Daladier was led to take over successively the portfolios of War, of Public Instruction and of Public Works.

It was always to the Ministry of War that he returned with the most enthusiasm. If he had decided ideas about the problems of the railroads, mining or of the schools, it was above all the national defense that most engaged his interest.

The experience in the war, the gaps and errors he had been able to observe from close range, filled him with an ardent desire to reorganize the army on the lines of a vast plan on which he had worked for years. But, unfortunately, ministerial instability did not permit him to carry through any comprehensive reorganization plan, and it was more as a deputy that he brought to the attention of the Chamber his plan of reorganization, destined to render the military forces more effective.

In Defense Of France

At that time a general loosening of fiber was possible in Europe. M. Daladier placed the politicians on guard:

"Do not," he recommended to them, "abandon the critical viewpoint. It is more necessary in the military domain than in any other."

He asked that Parliament give the country "an army strong, healthy, substantial, on a basis of one-year service." And he added:

"In our country, in order that a military institution be living and efficacious, it is necessary that it demand of the citizens only indispensable sacrifices, and that it be able by this means to obtain the co-operation of all to whom the appeal is made. For it is precisely such moderation that will bring them to perform their duties cheerfully."

At the same time circumstances led him to undertake the business of setting his party in order. He had been elected president of the Radical Socialist party in 1927. At that time it was necessary that he overcome certain tendencies that had manifested themselves, restore party unity, close up the cracks in the walls which threatened to bring the whole edifice down.

In the following year the method of election was changed. Deputies were voted on in the separate *arron-*

disements instead of on a general ticket for the *départe-ment*. M. Daladier presented himself before the electors in the *arrondisement* of Orange, in his native Vaucluse. They elected him.

Orange is only a few kilometers from Carpentras, but under that Provençal sky every town is in some sort a little local capital, possessing its own special character. Roman remains are much more prominent at Orange than anywhere else around the place. In the course of the centuries, instead of being either Papal or French like this or that of its neighbors, it was Protestant, and up to the time of Louis XIV it belonged to princes of the north.

Doubtless you are aware that the principality of Orange has given its name to two royal families, a republic in Central Africa and to several cities in the United States.

As its southerly climate is sunny most of the time, M. Daladier's political rallies were held, more frequently than not, out of doors, in the Ancient Theater which for two thousand years has stood at the foot of the hill of Orange, and whose benches, stepped up the flank of the hill, were covered with innumerable auditors.

In Defense Of France

It was before that Roman wall that, alluding to his own reputation for taciturnity, Edouard Daladier one day pronounced these words:

"I wish to recall once again the life of William of Orange, wrongly known as 'the Silent,' when he should have been called 'the Reticent.' He spoke only of what he knew well, and thus did not encounter the inconsistencies to which facile popularities lead. He had an intense interior life, the only resource that enables one to dominate the anger of men and the caprice of events."

It is by the exercise of the same qualities that Edouard Daladier has arrived at the same philosophy.

The elections of 1928 gave a majority to the Center parties in the Chamber of Deputies, but cutting across political difficulties, the President of the Republic appealed to the deputy from Orange in order to overcome the current crisis. Discovering that he would not be sustained by a majority as substantial as he wished, M. Daladier renounced the design of forming the cabinet over which he had been asked to preside.

Moreover, at this time he was occupied by family troubles. After having given birth to their second son, Mme Daladier had begun to show the symptoms of the illness which carried her off a few years later.

A Profile

Installed in the Ministry of War in December 1932, Edouard Daladier was at last able to attack the great task that was so dear to his heart. He undertook the labor of general reorganization in a sharply defensive sense, intending to demonstrate "that France will declare no war against any people, but that she is resolved to maintain her frontiers intact, to defend her territory, to assure her security, to prevent war again being made against her."

Coming out of the first meeting of the Superior Council of War over which he presided, the generals present declared they had never seen anyone take the chair with so much authority.

The minister could now go forward on a permanent basis; the whole army would follow him.

His specific acts were to bring about just and useful reforms, to reorganize the frontiers and to modernize the troops.

While pursuing his task as Minister of War, he was charged, in January 1933, with the task of constituting a new ministry. The papers had just announced that Adolf Hitler had seized power when they published the list of ministers in the Daladier cabinet, and while the new Chancellor of the Reich was taking possession of the streets of Berlin in the light of torches and flares, the

[29]

In Defense Of France

Prime Minister of France was working with his ministers in the peace of his office.

The tenacious and reflective will that he placed immediately at the service of the public brought him much support, for he gave a clear impression of being able to maintain all the interests of France as he had promised.

"Care for the republican patrimony, care for international peace"—these were the two objectives announced in his ministerial declaration; and it was with the intention of bringing about a loosening of European tension that he adopted the Four-Power Pact.

Emil Lengyel wrote in the New York *Times* at this time that Daladier was the champion of democracy, and asked what could have been accomplished without him, either at the Economic Conference of London or at the Disarmament Conference of Geneva. He continued:

"While Adolf Hitler is performing conspicuously on the German stage, Edouard Daladier is making world history without any dramatization of his personality and achievements. On his work much of Europe's hope depends."

And in these words he summed up his opinion of the man:

"His most marked characteristic is his belief in humanity."

A Profile

At the same time, if he sought to negotiate with the adversaries of France on the basis of the Four-Power Pact, Daladier did not intend to permit himself to be duped, and looking beyond the frontiers, he remarked that "if France is deaf to no word, she is also blind to no action."

Unfortunately German actions followed one another with mounting speed when Daladier left power, after February 1934.

At this time men of the "extreme Right," after having stirred public opinion by violent press campaigns and demonstrations in the streets, succeeded in attracting to their standards a sheeplike section of the Parisian public, demoralized by the economic depression. They exploited an incident with the intention of making the government—that is, the republic itself—responsible.

Thus France also passed through its little Fascist crisis.

In order to permit immediate appeasement of the domestic issue, Edouard Daladier offered the resignation of his ministry. He could now recall his words on William of Orange and fortify himself in his own silence.

The Doumergue ministry, which followed that of Daladier, adopted a new foreign policy. Nevertheless the general European situation continued to become more aggravated until May 1936, when the swing of the electoral pendulum brought in the Popular Front government.

The Radical Socialist party had engaged in the electoral battle in association with the other groups of the Left. For two years it had been the object of very violent attacks from the Right and Center, by which these latter hoped to defeat it and install themselves in its place. They accomplished no more than opening the path for the Socialists and bringing Léon Blum to the Prime Ministry.

M. Daladier, as a member of the Blum cabinet, was agreed with his chief in seeking to obtain more humane working conditions for members of the laboring class. From the very beginning of the Popular Front he declared himself on the side of the masses, peasants, laborers, men and women of the liberal professions, small industry and commerce, which have given to the Republic their hearts and their thoughts; he declared that he stood with the middle classes.

"It is because in other countries the middle classes have been reduced and robbed, sometimes wiped out, that dictatorship has been able to extend its shadow. Our duty to ourselves is to aid these classes, to protect them, liberate them, so that they may become the solid strength of the republican regime."

But the social laws, those crystallized aspirations of the workers, the generous enterprises of the government, "will not bear all their fruits," remarked M. Daladier, "unless they are executed in union, order and discipline; they demand vigilant attention, firm courage and voluntary forbearance from all. When the inevitable difficulties are waiting in our path, let us be frank enough to proclaim that the economic and social renovation of the country, the elevation of the purchasing power of the laboring classes, calls for the collaboration of all energies in mutual respect for republican order."

Laboring-class agitation, the persistent sit-down strikes, the war that broke out in Spain, lit every passion. M. Daladier, feeling the menace of the future spread out across Europe, became more and more deeply engaged in his work of national defense.

On returning to the Ministry of War in June 1936 he found before him the same problems as on the other occasions when he had held office, but by this time they had become much more grave and more difficult to solve. The minister took up his work at the point where he had left off in 1934, and applied himself to the task of giving the national defense new energy.

Charged with the duty of co-ordinating the military forces, he took over the whole national-defense problem (War, Navy and Air), creating a single command and for the first time achieving this rational centralization of all the defensive forces.

"National defense today goes beyond the limits of the plan of military organization," said he in his ministerial declaration when he once more assumed the functions of Prime Minister, in April 1938. "All financial, economic, social and political problems are narrowly linked with the problem of our security. There is no longer today a series of separate questions. There is only a unique problem, and the safety of the Country presents itself as a whole."

He therefore set to work without delay to stimulate economic activity. "We must get France back to work," said he. "We will have to do something about the forty-hour law."

Already, in October 1936, he had formulated certain reservations relative to the forty-hour week, to a system of labor which France, alone in Europe, was about to undertake. He set to work to get rid of the last relics of labor agitation in the factories.

A Profile

From the first weeks of his return to power, he made close contact with England in the course of a trip to London. He had earlier sought solutions at Geneva; but having discovered agreement impossible there, with the disarmament conference failing, the countries with which he had wished to negotiate resigning from the League of Nations, he had reached the conclusion that France could count on nothing but her own strength and her friendships.

He intensified and arranged this strength, after having elaborated a four-year plan to equip the army with perfected matériel, to create units for the defensive fortifications which reach from the North Sea to the Alps and border the Tunisian south.

At the same time he organized for officers the College of High Studies in National Defense, the Committee for the Production of War Materials, the Committee on Fuel, the Institute of Scientific Research, modernizing the army and adapting it to meet new necessities.

As to international friendships, he guarded them carefully, and he was, for example, able to address himself by radio to the American people with the certainty that they would understand him.

He might well have employed in regard to the Americans the same words he addressed to the King and Queen of England when they paid their visit to Paris:

"Every time a Frenchman speaks of France, he has the feeling he is expressing something that brings him nearer to other men. To speak of France is not for us a means of outlining a difference, and by means of this difference of seeking the evidence of an illusory superiority; on the contrary, it is to confide entirely in those whose friendship we wish.

"Nothing better expresses our feelings of heart and mind than to tell a foreigner, the friend who has come to visit us and who thinks of us across the frontiers, what our country and the men who inhabit it are like. The French peasant loves to open the door of his house and to set his table with the bread and wine of hospitality. He likes to do the honors of his fields and to pronounce the names of the forests, the hills, the watercourses which surround those fields.

"Like him, our savants, our writers, our philosophers and our men of action like to tell what France has accomplished in the course of the centuries.

"From the humblest to the most illustrious, from the peasant to the poet, they take the same way to attain the same friendship; the way of men who wish, as they do, labor in peace and dignity in justice."

A Profile

The speeches collected in this volume deal with the principal preoccupations of French policy from April 1938 to May 1939.

During these thirteen months the Prime Minister has voyaged among particularly dangerous reefs of foreign policy. Up to the end of September the feverishness of Europe mounted, and Munich afforded only a temporary relief to the growing agony of the peoples.

For several years now the world that listens in on the radio has been able to hear the leaders of nations speak before the microphone.

Voices which cross the frontiers frequently bring discordant vociferations to the ears. Ignorance of the language being spoken does not, nevertheless, prevent the auditor from forming some opinion of the man who is speaking. The timbre of his voice, the music of the language and, above all, his tone, furnish clues.

The world has heard Edouard Daladier speak. It has heard him address everything sane in the world, speaking from the intimacy of the little old salon in pale gold at Paris, where his working office as minister and as premier is installed—on the Rue Saint Dominique, with the office looking out over a little green garden.

In Defense Of France

His slow, grave voice shows him as the man "disdainful of charlatanisms"; weighing his words, he expresses himself with a firmness which veils his melancholy at being obliged to defend, foot by foot, the simplest ideas which, up to recent years, were the honor of the whole human race.

He has explained, as you know, "what France wants"; she wants the peace of free men, liberty to defend her ideals and her rights; she wants nothing else.

Premier Daladier will explain all this to you himself, in the course of these pages, very much better than I know how to explain it.

YVON LAPAQUELLERIE

(June 1939)

IN DEFENSE OF FRANCE

MINISTERIAL STATEMENT

A GREAT FREE COUNTRY can be saved only by its own efforts. The Government of National Defense which now stands before you is determined to be the expression of this will to live. Most of its ministers have played their part in the great popular movement which, in dark hours for democracy, affirmed a common will to defend the Republic and an equally ardent desire to provide social justice. They remain faithful to their ideal, their actions, their doctrine. With them some loyal and sincere republicans who, setting aside party differences, quite recently were declaring their decision to collaborate, in a vast national assembly, are ready to face the dangers and difficulties of the present hour. All strongly united, we appeal to Parliament and the nation for the defense of liberty, of country and of peace.

Immediately around us and farther beyond our borders Europe is undergoing a transformation. New ideologies now move vast populations. Some states disappear while new empires are born. That is why national defense today goes beyond the limits of the plan of military organization. All financial, economic, social and

[41]

political problems are narrowly linked with the problem of our security. There is no longer today a series of separate questions. There is only a unique problem, and the safety of the country presents itself as a whole.

National defense, then, requires a sound currency, finance that does not bear the mark of weakness that may soon become fatal. The resort to exceptional and temporary measures is permissible only if it is followed by general measures which at last get to the core of the evil that, for the last twenty years, has worked such havoc in our midst.

National defense requires also vigorous economics. It cannot admit any slowing or stoppage in production, especially in the industries concerned with the safety of the country.

That is why the government appeals to the wisdom and patriotism of workmen and employers. Workmen must realize that stay-in-strikes in factories give the whole of the country a feeling of anxiety which may become, as has happened in other nations, a danger to liberty itself.

Employers must loyally obey the labor laws which they themselves have declared they considered final. From now on, all disputes can be settled within the framework of the law by a procedure of conciliation and arbitration. Moreover, the government will submit to the vote of the two Houses the texts, now under consideration, that will complete these modern labor statutes.

But the government, mindful only of the national interest, will see to it that there is no delay in the production of arms necessary to the security of the country—arms without which France would be a prey to invasion.

National defense also implies defense of the Republic. To the steps that the government will take to insure it will correspond, we are convinced, the effort of recovery—confident, cheerful, irresistible—which, coming from the very depths of our rural and city populations, will safeguard the necessary unity of France.

Lastly, and above all, national defense implies the defense of peace. Without renouncing the noble principles with which, during the Great War, over millions of dead, we had sworn to build up true peace, the government is determined to defend everywhere the interests of France and the integrity of her empire. It will not allow threats to cast a shadow over her frontiers, her lines of communication, her colonies. It will not permit foreign influences, unrest caused by undesirable foreigners, to interfere with the entire liberty of its decisions.

In Defense Of France

Whether to strengthen her friendships, to prove her loyalty to all pacts and treaties that she has signed, or to play her part in just negotiations, it is indispensable for her to insure the cohesion of all national energies.

We want peace with all peoples, whatever their form of government, but peace in the respect of right, and not in a sort of abdication which would be for us a sure forerunner of servitude.

For this work of public safety, the government appeals to the noble sentiment of French fraternity that always has saved the country. Ours are methods of freedom. They will justify the discipline and the effort we shall exact from all. The hour has come to prove that France can face the dangers which threaten her while remaining faithful to her genius.

We shall ask the nation to make possible one of those miracles of liberty and reason whose long succession illuminates our history. We shall ask you, gentlemen [members of the Chamber of Deputies], to think clearly of the grandeur and permanence of the destiny with which, like us, you are entrusted.

April 13, 1938.

[44]

STABILITY OF THE FRANC

STABILITY OF THE FRANC

THE GOVERNMENT which I formed three weeks ago was from the outset wrestling with two great difficulties requiring an immediate solution. It was imperative first to restore social order, peace among Frenchmen. The government has, therefore, settled labor disputes. The great strikes have come to an end, thanks to the spirit of conciliation between employer and employed, and work has started again.

The second difficulty concerned our relations with foreign countries. It was due to the divisions of European countries, causing each one to arm against the other instead of following a policy of coalescence. At the London conference, because I was supported by your will to face all perils, I was able, with the collaboration of Georges Bonnet, to strengthen the sincere and loyal entente between France and Great Britain, guarantee of freedom and peace.

Scarcely back from London, I had to face economic and financial difficulties. As always, I will tell the country the whole truth.

Here is that truth:

[47]

In Defense Of France

The truth is that our economic life is deeply perturbed; that legitimate profit shows a tendency to disappear; that partial unemployment is increasing in business concerns; that our commercial balance is impoverishing us; that our rate of production remains a cause of humiliation for the French people.

The truth is that with this drained economic life, the national budget inevitably shows a deficit; that the needs of the Treasury exhaust national savings, deteriorate public credit, dry up private credit, threatening financial stability.

The government responsible for the destinies of the country cannot allow so grave a situation to continue.

There can be no question of doctrines or experiments.

Whether orthodox or bold, generous or cruel, any measure that is directly linked with public safety is necessary, any measure which has no direct bearing on the situation is superfluous.

Such is the spirit behind the course of action which we have decided to take.

The foundation of this action is the appeal to the confidence of the country.

But, to pursue a lasting policy of confidence, we have to fix a strong base line that will resist all attacks. We must first fix a monetary basis that will correspond to our expenditure, that cannot be continually questioned, and that will put the franc at last beyond the attacks which for years have been launched against it.

That is why, despite adverse criticism, I have decided to bring back our currency and to put the franc on a basis where it will be adequately defended.

The French government, in full agreement with the American and British governments, whom I thank for their cordial and loyal collaboration, has, therefore, resolved to establish an adjustment of the franc at a rate insuring its victorious defense. This decision has been taken within the limits of the tripartite agreement to which the French government remains firmly attached.

The rate I have fixed for tomorrow will not fall lower. People will then be able to invest their savings in our national currency without fearing any new devaluation; rather will they anticipate a recovery of the franc. Thus shall we be enabled to pursue the work of reconstruction that imposes upon all Frenchmen an effort that must nevertheless remain their own choice.

The next government loan for national defense will give the French people an opportunity of taking the plebiscite of their patriotism with the full knowledge of the facts. Moreover, the decrees that have been published must not be considered only in their fiscal aspect, unpleasant but necessary, of an increase in taxes. They form a whole program of measures which favor the development of production and exchanges, currency circulation, the execution of important works and the opening of vast wood-, timber-, coal- and dockyards, and which are connected with the whole of national life, since these measures affect not only our great cities but also our most remote villages.

We are putting before you this plan that will prevent our currency from having to sustain continual attacks and will permit it to protect the gold reserve necessary to national defense.

We have preferred to appeal to the courage of the French people rather than allow ourselves to drift towards breakers.

Our supreme goal is to develop French labor. The law of democracy is the law of effort.

No new variations in currency, no new expenditure, no extra burdens. Peace at home, condition of peace abroad—that is what we want. There is no need for many words to convey to Frenchmen that the time has come for them to make a concerted effort for the return of discipline and work.

Speech broadcast May 4, 1938.

THE CALL TO WORK

THE FORTY-HOUR LAW

CLASHES OF ARMS and international differences are at the present time the prevalent preoccupations of the peoples. War rages in Spain and the Far East. In Central Europe some great nations take stock of their military strength or experiment with it. For their soldiers and reserves there is no longer any real limit to the duration of military service. For their workmen there is no longer any real limit to the hours of work. Most countries in the world also give the same evidence of intense activity. All these facts should be a warning to France.

I have told you before that I did not believe in the inevitability of war. Like all war veterans, I am resolved to do anything to prevent the destruction of European civilization. You also know that we have organized our own forces to put them at the service of our will for peace. We have again perfected them and decided upon measures that will increase them. No one in the world is underestimating their material and moral power. Lastly, you are aware of the ties of friendship and community of interests that unite us to great democracies moved, like France, by the same ardent desire for freedom.

But that is not enough. National defense has to be considered as a whole. The strength of a country, the guarantee of its independence, are proved not only by its military power, but at least as much by its daily effort at the factory, in the workroom, in every timber- and dockyard in the country, by the stability of its currency and the flourishing condition of its finances. Peace with honor, solidarity with the great democracies of the world, we can only maintain to the extent of the courage we will show to avoid any monetary and financial crisis. I am convinced that a new devaluation of the franc, or the establishment of control over the rates of exchange, which is another form of devaluation, would immediately render precarious, if not ruin, the international agreements which I have just mentioned. I am equally certain that a monetary and financial crisis in France— and I am quoting here the evidence of the best qualified observer in this field—"would be considered as a favorable circumstance by those who want war."

Our duty then is to avoid a crisis that would be full of perils both for France and peace.

The Forty-Hour Law

But, you may retort, what facts warrant the belief in the possibility of this crisis?

From the point of view of traditional monetary technique, is not the franc one of the strongest currencies in the world, since, if we take into account the actual value in francs today of the reserve and of the equalization fund, which, from the moment of legal stabilization, will be incorporated into our reserves? The coverage behind circulating money will then be about 100 per cent. At that very moment loans from the Bank of France to the Treasury would be completely redeemed, leaving a balance of several billions of francs to the credit of the State.

On the other hand, are there not a great number of figures and facts that show the confidence of France in her own destiny? The return to our country of a capital of several billions of francs, the great surplus of deposits in the savings banks, the continual increase of the monthly receipts of the State, the large subscriptions to Treasury bonds and National Defense bonds, the settlement of a series of important debts falling due, without having recourse to loans from the Bank of France—are not all these as many proofs of confidence?

All this is correct. However, in spite of all these favorable facts, for some days, in this atmosphere of international complications that have weighed heavily on the world's markets, why has France shown herself more nervous, more emotional than could have been foreseen from her previous confidence and her recent hopes? Why, on the French and foreign markets, have people doubted the stability of the franc, the future of our currency?

The essential reason, which unfortunately is scarcely mentioned in our country, is that the national revenue of France has gradually decreased for some years, while the expenditure of the State, in its various departments, was constantly increasing. In 1914 the French national revenue was 38 billions of gold francs. In 1931 it rose to 49 billions. In 1937 it had fallen to 22 billions, from which expenditure of the State, in its various departments, had made a previous deduction of 10 billions. Let us add, so as to make this a still more striking lesson, that incomes derived from work, wages, salaries, pensions, have on the whole kept very nearly their bullion value of prewar days. Incomes derived from land and houses and from investments show a decrease of 45 per cent. Mixed incomes, that is to say incomes derived from investment of capital in labor, in agricultural, industrial and commercial enterprises, have decreased by 66 per cent.

The road to salvation is, then, straight before us. We must increase the national revenue. We must put France back to work. Certainly, revision of public expenditure is necessary, and I have decided to create the organization whose control and initiative will ascertain where economies must be made. We are also determined to make a vigorous effort to balance the budget and to compress with energy supplementary estimates. But I will never propose a policy of sterile deflation that has repeatedly been proved powerless. I am not asking the French for sacrifices. I am asking them for a more vigorous, resolute and tenacious effort, with the aim of restoring activity, increasing production, creating new capital and improving the country's resources in proportion to the burdens that any modern state is compelled to bear for its administration as well as its defense.

We must first adapt the forty-hour law to the national necessities as well as to the general situation in Europe. In no country in the world, except France and Mexico, is this the normal rule of labor. In no country in the world do they leave idle one or two days a week the very machinery created to save man's labor. As long as the international situation remains so unsettled, we must be enabled to work more than forty hours and even up to forty-eight in enterprises concerned with national defense. And in any enterprise that needs it, it is imperiously necessary that it be able to dispose not only of forty hours a week but of all the hours necessary to its activity, without any useless formalities or endless discussions. There is no question of repealing the forty-hour law, but all enterprises that can do so must be allowed to work overtime. At the same time, extra hours of work ought not to be paid at the present prohibitive rates, but according to a reasonable scale that can certainly vary with the different industries, but which ought not to exceed 10 per cent more on an average.

Now that she is faced with totalitarian states which, regardless of the hours of work, arm and equip themselves, and is faced also with democratic states which, in an endeavor to recover their prosperity or insure their security, have adopted the forty-eight-hour week, will France, poorer and more threatened than any, spend any more time in controversies that endanger her future?

This increased effort—which is not a sacrifice, but a source of comfort for workers—I am also asking from employers. They have to provide a more rational organization in their enterprises, a real improvement of their methods, and a more up-to-date plant. With the same regard for social peace, they must respect the laws that have added dignity to labor.

In these conditions it will become possible for the State to help production, especially in removing the burden of some excessive taxes that weigh heavily on industry. The government, foreseeing this necessity, will deal with it by means of a decree which will at once come into force. I am convinced that relieving this burden will help to control the rising prices and to restore profit which is a source of revenue for the State and engenders private wealth. The stability of cost prices as well as selling prices is, moreover, an imperative necessity. Incessant rise would bring about the fatal reduction of the people's standard of living and would also be a mortal threat to the franc.

In the line of action that I am resolved to follow from the threefold point of view of work, economics and finance, I am determined to avoid the constantly recurring conflict between the needs of public credit and those of private concerns. Normal tax returns and the number of subscriptions to the short-term loan must be, for the present, sufficient for the current needs of the Treasury. The State, then, is determined to leave part of the country's revenue to private business. Funds allocated to overhead expenses of business have been drained by the increase of charges and the rising prices; sinking funds and more especially investments have been found insufficient. Business must be able to borrow capital at a reasonable rate. The economic strength of France is an essential element of her prestige and her staying power.

This will lead me, no doubt, in the near future, to give you some concrete details about the development of a plan of which I have been able tonight to give you only a brief outline, for fear of making this speech too long. You will not doubt my words if I add that I am guided by a single care, I ought to say a single passion: the security and grandeur of France. Let all Frenchmen, in view of the European and world situation, call a truce to their unimportant differences, let them accomplish the effort urgently needed to save their country. Let us send France back to work and we shall save peace. Let us send France back to work and we can rest assured of the stability of labor legislation founded upon justice. Let us send France back to work and we shall be able, with stabilized prices, to realize other generous reforms to which I am as deeply attached as anyone. It is in view of this defense of France and her security that we must pursue a firm policy of recovery, with confidence and discipline and the ardent desire for peace and for the achievement of her national destiny.

Speech broadcast August 21, 1938.

AN APPEAL TO THE COMMON SENSE
OF THE FRENCH PEOPLE

O<small>N</small> THURSDAY, November 24—four days ago—Mr Chamberlain and Lord Halifax, in the name of the British government, were studying, with the French government, in a spirit of confidence and friendship, the problems of the common defense of Great Britain and France, as well as the safest means of securing peace for Europe. At the same time, cessation of work and brutal stay-in strikes were suddenly declared in Paris and in the departments of Nord and Seine-Inférieure.

On Friday, November 25, to the announcement of the impending signature of a double declaration by France and Germany for the mutual respect of their frontiers, came the reply within twenty-four hours of the threat of a general strike.

Why these stay-in strikes, which have been declared illegal by all successive heads of governments since 1936? Why this general strike, from which only the most humble citizens will have to suffer? Why this appeal to civil servants who are incited to transgress republican law by forming a coalition to paralyze all public

[62]

services? Why these orders to prevent all trains from leaving, beginning with 4 A.M. Tuesday, to block all signals and to abandon on sidings all French and foreign passengers from that time on?

The pretext is to protest against the decrees, against what is called destruction of labor legislation. It is for the representatives of the nation who gave me the necessary powers, and for them alone, to decide before the 31st of December whether or not these decrees are to be repealed. It is for Parliament alone to say whether France, incapable of the vigorous effort of recovery that all the democracies of the world have freely accomplished, will fall back into the groove of a life from which effort is banished, or if she will recover her prestige in the world by her courage and energy.

As to the so-called destruction of labor legislation, did we ever repeal paid holidays, threaten salaries, suppress the forty-hour week? This last only needs to be adapted —an engagement that all my predecessors had undertaken—to the necessities of French economic life and the requirements of national defense.

All these are absurd pretexts. There is really no moral justification at all for the general strike which French workers are now urged to declare. Public liberties are

[63]

not threatened by anyone. It is a ridiculous invention to speak, as some are trying to do, of dictatorship and fascism. Dictatorship, in fact, does not consist in asking from the country the necessary sacrifices for the life of the nation, through legal means and with respect for republican laws: it consists in imposing the will of a party or a clan by violent means, in bringing pressure to bear on the population of a country and its legal government by first resorting to a kind of blackmail before the supreme recourse to force.

I am determined to end such methods and resolutely to secure the respect of all for the laws of the Republic.

Let us be clear and frank. These sudden stay-in strikes, partial strikes, and the general strike are an attempt at brutal action against the policy of peace pursued by the government, which is as careful as anyone of the honor and dignity of France and mindful above all not to shed French blood for the sake of interests that are not those of France. These threats and stay-in strikes, suddenly started, this call for a general strike, are, in fact, whether it is admitted or kept in the background, an attempt of force by the dictatorship of a minority over the mass of the people and the republican democracy.

What happened on Thursday night at the Renault

Appeal To Common Sense Of French People
works confirms in the most striking way what I have
just told you. There was no professional cause for the
cessation of work and the sudden occupation of the
buildings by workmen. Neither conditions of work nor
salaries were in question. But the pamphlets, posters and
orders that have been circulated all over the works be-
trayed the political origin of the movement.

It was and still is a question of launching a mass attack against the government of the Republic, as some
chiefs of international organizations had let us know in
their aggressive speeches, and as some of their papers
had warned us in their passionate attacks. It was and still
is a question of forcing us to come to terms under
threats. I need not tell you that the government is ab-
solutely resolved to do its duty towards the nation.

But I want to address myself to the reason and conscience of all Frenchmen. I ask them to think of the
disastrous consequences that a period of disorders would
have upon the destiny of our country.

Not a single French worker can hope to benefit by it
in any way. All workers would be, on the contrary, the
deplorable victims. French workmen know that their
material conditions are better than those of the workmen of the great nations which surround us. They know

[65]

that labor legislation is not threatened. They understand that they have themselves the greatest interest in the prosperity of France, the condition necessary for the happiness of all her sons.

It is to the union of all Frenchmen, without any class or creed distinction, that the government appeals, to their common sense, their reason, their devotion to the public good.

While dictatorship has gradually thrown its shadow over the whole world, France, faithful to her genius, remains the land of liberty.

Frenchmen, do not jeopardize your liberty, do not cast a blow at the dignity and grandeur of France by helping or tolerating fruitless insurrections. Remain united for the salvation of all.

I have indeed been distressed by the organization of this activity, which can only be harmful to the life of the nation. But if, in spite of my efforts, these threats are followed by actions, I will do my duty, all my duty, with the certainty that I am right, since I have no other thought but to insure the respect of the law and to protect the great interests of the country.

Speech broadcast Sunday evening, November 27, 1938.

FAILURE OF THE GENERAL STRIKE

THE FORESIGHT AND PATRIOTISM of the French people have just been affirmed once more in a striking way.

The 30th of November was to be a historical date. A general strike was to demonstrate the brutal opposition of the country to the policy of reason and peace that the government pursues indefatigably, both in international relations and in the country itself. The whole life of the nation was to be paralyzed while our opponents watched with irony, and our friends throughout the world, with great sadness.

In the evening of this day I have the right to say that the 30th of November will, as a matter of fact, remain a historical date. The complete failure of the general strike shows the confidence of the country and its determination to collaborate with the government to enforce respect of the law and so insure the safety of France.

I need not describe to you the events of the day. The French are observant. Trains have run as usual. Post-office, telegraph and telephone services have functioned normally. Children have found schools open. In the

In Defense Of France

Parisian district there has been the normal amount of traffic in underground services and general transport. There has been no interference with any of the vital activities of the country. In private industry itself, cessation of work has only been partial. There have been no serious disturbances. I was certain there would not be. I was able to form my conviction after I had read the thousands of telegrams and letters that you sent me after my speech of Sunday evening. You are always understood by the French if you address yourself to the clear mind of the people.

I had said that I would have the law of the Republic respected. It has been. I had said that I would not tolerate the stoppage of public services. They have not stopped. I had placed my confidence in workmen and civil servants and trusted them to gain a victory over propaganda harmful to the country. They have answered my call. They were able on their own to gain the upper hand because they felt they were supported and protected by the government and by the laws of the Republic. Such has been their part. Such has been the part I have wanted to play. It is not for the head of the government of France to gain a victory over some misled Frenchmen, but it is his duty to see that those making mad attempts that would lead the country to its ruin are prevented from carrying out their plan.

Today's triumph is that of the very principle both of the Republic and of liberty: The respect of law, work and country.

The workers of France had been told that they had to stop work to defend labor legislation. The people of France have answered. They have proved by their attitude that they knew labor legislation to be safe. We have left intact paid holidays, salaries, the forty-hour law. We have, as our predecessors had promised to do, wisely adapted this law to the exigencies of production and national defense.

The people of France have, above all, shown that they knew their liberty was not in question. For you had been told some unreliable tale of a threat to your liberty. But I know you well, and I feel sure you have understood that, on the contrary, what could imperil your liberty was disorder and indiscipline. You remember, because of your experience as free men, that it was precisely the upheaval of general strikes which, in other countries, opened the door to dictators. You remember that it was thanks to anarchy, in the internal conflicts between people of the same land, that the rhythmic step of marching legions was first heard.

In Defense Of France

You have understood that the guarantee of freedom is the law of the State. And that is why you have refused to strike blows against this Republic that has been the first founder of your liberty and remains its guardian. You have not forgotten that trade unionism itself is the product of the Republic and that in France it is not the mob, but the people, who have sovereignty.

Lastly, you have understood that a single day of disorder would lower the prestige of France in the world and that the safest means of insuring peace and the respect of our rights was to demonstrate our power of union and work.

This morning foreign papers were still asking themselves, some with a friendly anxiety, others with a cheerful hope, what this day would bring to France. "Democracy shows itself. powerless to check disorder and anarchy," said some. You have proved that democracy, when it wishes, prevents the outbreak of disturbances and the spreading of anarchy.

The whole world already knows that France has triumphed over her internal difficulties and that she is stronger today than yesterday.

Tomorrow, with her freedom saved, her moral unity recovered, France will pursue her effort. The union of all her sons is indispensable. I have always felt certain myself of seeing it realized. It is the wish of the entire nation. The government will not disappoint this hope. It has called a halt to the internal divisions that might have struck a death blow. It will know how to organize productive collaboration between workmen and employers in a spirit of mutual understanding and respect for our laws.

Thus, with French fraternity restored, our country will become nobler and prouder, and each Frenchman will be able to find happiness and peace in the cheerful fulfillment of his duty.

Speech broadcast November 30, 1938.

APPEASEMENT

THE DIFFICULT TIMES that France has to face demand the reconciliation of all Frenchmen. When peril is at our door, we must think only of the country. The union of all her sons is the condition of her safety.

That is why I address myself today to employers and employed.

After the strike of the 30th of November, the chiefs of some enterprises, exercising their full right, refused to take back a certain number of workers who had, as a matter of fact, wrongly denounced their contract. I am asking French employers, in circumstances calling for the mobilization of all hearts as well as all hands, to arrange for the immense majority of the strikers of the 30th of November to find their place again in the national production.

The State itself will offer employment on a large scale to the workers with whom it had been necessary to part.

I am convinced that employers will do the same, either taking back the greatest possible number of workmen who had been dismissed, or endeavoring to get them employment in similar concerns. They will thus follow the noblest traditions of French generosity.

And I also trust that workers who were dismissed and who will find their posts again at the factory or the dockyard will make every effort to increase the national output, which in view of the present European situation must be pushed on full speed ahead for the defense of the country.

Statement to the press, March 23, 1939.

TWO FRIENDSHIPS OF FRANCE

FRANCO–SWISS FRIENDSHIP

IN YOUR SPEECH, which was so moving, loyal and sincere, you have succeeded in reconciling Jean-Jacques Rousseau and Voltaire. You have shown the happily married Voltaire's subtle irony and Jean-Jacques Rousseau's admirable depth of thought. Modern Switzerland is reflected there. Your country, in fact, offers the really moving spectacle of a nation where live, in perfect harmony, men who belong to the great races who share Europe, men who belong to religions that have often been antagonistic, men who speak different languages.

You give, at the same time, the spectacle of the reconciliation of all classes. Switzerland thus bears witness to that great reconciliation of humanity to which Frenchmen, whatever their political creed, have devoted their thought and their activity.

Switzerland is a great country because she has been able to group men of all origins, all religions, around one central idea: the interest of their country. It is your grandeur, and it is the example you give us.

As minister of national defense, it was my duty to

think of what you call your western frontier. For my duty is to prepare France to be ready to defend herself on all frontiers.

I have been through the zone which has been de-militarized since the Battle of Waterloo, since the treaty of 1815. I have seen regions that belong to France, but where she is not allowed to build fortifications because the Allies who beat Napoleon forbade her to do so in 1815. From the military point of view, such a situation is a drawback for France, but after having scoured the country and after reflection, I said to myself: "What do a few kilometers matter for the installation of our batteries and our posts of observation! All these precautions would have only a relative and secondary importance, for there lives a great friendly people which has given us during the Great War the measure of its loyal friendship."

I am happy, then, to have been in full agreement with M. Motta. I ask you to address my best regards to him, assuring him of my understanding.

May I be allowed to say that the example you set, which is the fruit of the experience of several centuries, deserves much meditation on the part of statesmen and would tend to instill in them an attitude of modesty?

Franco-Swiss Friendship

We have, in France, only one wish. It is that your country continue to live in this unity, that she may be a living lesson in the heart of Europe, a moving protest against those who would subject humanity's destiny to racial hatreds and religious antagonism, when the aim of our modern civilization should be to reconcile all races, to create harmony between all religions.

In the times in which we are now living, our duty is to utilize for the common good all French qualities, as well as everything else that may be either complementary or different in the make-up of our people, following the example given by Switzerland.

I think I shall not be contradicted by anyone if I declare that Europe, democracy and the ideal of liberty are narrowly linked with the existence and the grandeur of our country. The mission of the provincial newspapers represented here dictates the most imperative and absolute duty to you all, gentlemen, who form the daily press. This duty you have already understood. Liberty is an absolute condition of the life of the press in a democratic country.

Whatever the political party you represent, in whichever part of France your paper appears, I feel nothing but friendship for you. I quite understand that you should discuss the men in the government; it is your right. I know that the great provincial papers never derive their inspiration from base interests, are not motivated by base reasons, but are guided by healthy ideals which are in conformity with the interest of France.

I know that, though I speak here to a small gathering, I am also speaking to men who represent one of the great potentialities of the country. For I know well these daily provincial papers. I have been and am their collaborator; I, too, have written in these regional papers, to their evident pleasure, because they are the only papers that have never passed any remark on the expression of my convictions, nor ever asked me to change so much as a comma. The regional daily papers are the very mirror of France. That is where ideas take shape that can be discussed, ideas that have constructive value and may sometimes be decisive. I will never ask the papers you represent to be either favorable or unfavorable to the government of which I am prime minister, I simply ask them always to tell me the truth as they see it. If, at times, their criticisms are a little too vigorous, I find in them an exercise for testing my power of reaction or reflex. I never entertain any resentment for them.

This free criticism is one of the foundations of French

strength. Thanks to its impetus, our public opinion was built stone by stone, slowly, strongly. And if our nation, through so many obstacles, so many difficulties, has always kept its freedom, it is because it has safeguarded it throughout the diversity of its provinces. This is the spirit that has enabled it to save liberty, whenever it was imperiled, whether on the Marne or at Verdun. I have, therefore, only to ask you to continue your work in each of your French provinces, so that there may be more and more understanding between Frenchmen.

When you examine the differences which sometimes render our task so delicate, you come to realize that there are practically never any technical questions in the way, that it is not a question of mean interests, but of misunderstanding between Frenchmen. What we have to bring back, then, is the spirit of harmony and solidarity among the French. France is a democracy: you represent her. If, in some foreign papers, we read that she is again a land of privileges, a gloomy country, anxious for her future, solely preoccupied by base interests, it is no longer a picture, it is a caricature! I am asking you to give the lie to this caricature, in the interest of Europe herself.

I am rather like the peasant who wanted to give ad-

vice to his vicar. I do not want to give advice to the
canons of the provincial press, I am merely asking them
to accentuate this angle, so that Frenchmen may re-
discover and understand the immense latent strength that
is in them, so that they may know that in the present
European conditions the world expects a great people
like ours to raise its voice in words that will carry a
meaning of strength and peace. Let us find again the
route to Switzerland, to meet on the way Voltaire, re-
dresser of wrongs, and Jean-Jacques Rousseau, builder
of a new society. Rest assured that everything can be
righted, everything can be restored, that foreign peoples
who heap sarcasms upon us do not realize the immortal
strength that is in us. Let us accomplish our task as
Frenchmen, that is to say, the task of men who have a
regard for truth, who know that their country can only
fulfill the hopes that other peoples may have in her
destiny if they themselves give an example of union,
harmony and fraternity.

*Speech delivered May 17, 1938, at the luncheon given
by the Association of Daily Provincial Newspapers for
M. Stucki, Swiss minister in Paris, and members of the
Swiss colony.*

FRANCO–AMERICAN FRIENDSHIP

It is a great pleasure for me today, in the name of the government of the Republic, to pay the homage of the French people to the memory of George Washington.

For you Americans, as for us French, the national inheritance is made up both of a material and a moral reality: a land which we love, and a high ideal of fraternity, liberty and justice to which we are even more strongly attached.

George Washington was the hero who consolidated and freed the territories that make up your country, but he was, at the same time, the founder of your democracy. He is, then, both the most American and the most universal of your great men, and it is by right of this double mission that he deserves our admiration and our gratitude.

Gathered here to celebrate his memory, we know that we are still—all of us—actuated by the spirit of justice and liberty that guided him in all his enterprises. Because of that, I know that I can address myself to the

[83]

whole American people with the certainty of being understood. At this moment, when my voice is carried over the vast Atlantic and across the far-flung States, I feel that I am no longer speaking to a foreign people but to men of my own country whom I know personally and who cannot misunderstand the meaning of yes and no.

It is the privilege of free peoples to be able to understand one another in this way, across oceans, in spite of all distances and differences that may separate them. If we are sure to be able to understand each other, it is because we—all of us—give the same value to the same words and because we like and desire the same things.

The thought that seems to us most worth expressing is the affirmation of our will for peace and our hope to see it well established in spite of all the perils that threaten it.

French or Americans, we have in fact only one and the same policy: that which consists in maintaining peace. Geographical and historical circumstances may give our actions different aspects: but our will remains identical. All of us are seeking peace in work and honor. We are seeking peace because we are democrats, because nothing is more precious to us than freedom and human dignity, because we do not wish any glory for our countries other than the possibility of making a little more happiness for those who work and toil.

But, for the very reason that we are democrats, we cannot admit peace without honor. We are opposed to the idea of war because we are both human and reasonable, because we think it is absurd and criminal to sacrifice human beings and to accumulate material ruins, because we know beforehand that war cannot bring any lasting solution to any of the problems that confront us. But it is precisely because we think all this that we cannot resign ourselves to any surrender. Peace and liberty are for us inseparable possessions. We could not agree to pay for the one by the loss of the other. Our love of peace is not a sign of weakness or cowardice. It is the result of a reasonable decision. It is the crowning point in all our thought as free and civilized men.

We want peace and we want the means of peace. These means are, in our judgment, the very means of democracy: the mutual respect of individuals and groups, of the sacred character of liberty, the pooling of everything that can contribute to the material and moral elevation of humanity. But such an action implies the renunciation by all of recourse to violence, the acknowledgment by all of the sacred laws that must govern human intercourse: respect of man for man, respect of the pledged word, respect of the weak, and lastly, self-respect that excludes the resort to force for any other service than that of justice.

That is why, in a deeply perturbed world, we have to remain vigilant and to put ourselves in the position to resist all threats and attacks.

Need I tell you this evening, American friends, that France will never yield to threats of force or to cunning blackmail? She will not tolerate anyone interfering with her inheritance, with what has been gathered and conquered by the effort of the French and which, in the very spirit of democracy, has always been wide open, to the effort of all men of good will. In her far-flung empire France has welcomed all men who wanted to work with her for the common good.

France offers a welcome, indeed, but she is resolved to secure the respect of her rights. When it is a question of the independence of our country and the integrity of our land, we are resolved to face all threats. That is why we will firmly maintain union between Frenchmen and devote all our strength to the defense of the nation. But we remain no less determined to participate, with reciprocal loyalty and with an efficacious control, in any feasible policy for both the limitation and the reduction of armaments.

We have not given up the dream of someday seeing humanity devote to works of life an effort, as large and complete, as the one it now devotes to works of death. The centuries-old civilization of France and the youthful civilization of her Empire have within them all the necessary powers for such an enterprise. What an outburst of enthusiasm throughout the world would welcome such an effort! And what could we not expect from you, American friends, who have already contributed so much to the technical and moral civilization of our time, you who, for so many years, in the midst of the upheavals of a world where insanity seems sometimes to be sovereign, have stood as a bulwark for peace, have made the world echo with words of wisdom and of peace!

Today our armed vigilance remains the rampart of this dream. Our first duty is to prevent, by the reality of our force, the world from being swept into situations implicit with danger. If we overcome a few difficulties which are immediately ahead of us, then we shall be able to undertake a great work of progress.

For all these tasks of peace, we know that we should

In Defense Of France

have—that we *have*—a joint responsibility. It is not necessary for us to be bound by texts or promises to work together for what seems to us the good of humanity. There is no need for us to pledge our word to each other. Our word is pledged by the very fact that we all serve the same cause: that of liberty and justice.

Today, when we celebrate the memory of a man whose virtues appeal as much to the French as to Americans, allow me, Mr Ambassador—you who have, by virtue of your position among us, linked our country to yours with so much cordial vision and firm courage—allow me to raise my glass in your honor.

Together, French and Americans, we will address a salute to President Roosevelt, who is one of the guiding spirits in the world's will for peace and who gives our France so many proofs of affectionate solicitude. Let him know, Mr Ambassador, that at the present time there is not a Frenchman, however humble, who, when dreaming of peace, does not evoke the image of the President of the United States and turn to him with hope.

It is to the whole American people as well as to President Roosevelt that we wish tonight to dedicate the homage of our gratitude and our affection. The people

[88]

of France are grateful to them for being both the strongest and the most peaceful nation in the world, the most attached to social and economic progress and the most careful of moral values.

I raise my glass to peace, to President Roosevelt, who has set himself the task of defending it, and to the whole American people.

Speech delivered at the dinner given in commemoration of the birth of George Washington, February 22, 1939.

SALUTE TO THE AMERICANS

THE MEN WHOSE MEMORY we are honoring today are not the heroes of a closed epoch. Doubtless they already belong to history, but they are also men of our own time. If their lives had followed the normal course they would now be men of our age. They partook of our labors and our cares. They partook also of our hopes, and their desires accorded with ours.

Thus it is not in speaking of death before their tombs that we will remain faithful to their spirit. On the contrary, it is by addressing a message of life to those who have survived them. These dead of our own generation, these dead who could be the guides and inspiration of our time—they ask us to do what they would have done were they still among us. They ask us to be the guardians of that which they desired to save by their sacrifice. They ask us to be the servants of life.

For it is not of death they thought, these young men who disembarked in our Atlantic ports in the spring of 1917 to fight in France. They thought of the future.

[90]

They wished to build a world in which peace and justice would finally reign.

Old soldiers of the war, such as we were then, harassed by months of suffering, rediscovered beside these young soldiers the enthusiasm that had sent them marching to the front of peril in 1914. The Americans brought to the poilus of Verdun a magnificent certainty. By their mere presence they declared that life would have the strength to continue after the terrible test. They restored the hope of youth.

The operations of the American army on the front in France could legitimately take the name of "the offensive of hope." For if Verdun was the battle of resolution, Saint-Mihiel and Montfaucon were the battles of hope. That hope was not one of victory alone. It looked toward a future wider and still more fecund of hope. It announced to all, in the mud of the trenches and under the shellbursts, that beyond the conflict a new life was about to begin: the life of free men who expected nothing but what their labor had to give them.

For more than twenty years now our dead have been reposing in their glory, and we may ask ourselves whether we have remained faithful to the spirit which animated them. The brutal force which they wished to crush is more threatening than ever. Justice and liberty are in peril. Have we then been unworthy guardians of their heritage?

I am thinking of the American women who lost a son, a husband, a fiancé in the war; I am thinking of the Americans who did not see the return of the dear ones who marched away under the star-spangled banner. I recognize their right to demand of us what we have done with all this suffering and all this sacrifice. I seem to hear their voices from beyond the ocean, demanding of old Europe what it has gained from this formidable test; I seem to hear the terrible question which rises from the depths of their being: "Are you worthy of the blood spilled and of the examples which have been set for you?"

It is to this question that I wish to reply, standing here before this monument which recalls at the same time the supreme sacrifice of so many sons of the United States and the profound reasons which led them to accept death at the side of the sons of France, of Great Britain and of all their allies.

The events through which we have just been living could be a challenge to the spirit of our dead; the world of today could be considered the opposite of the world they wished to make; the dreams they formed could be thought to correspond in no degree with the hard reality which surrounds us; nevertheless, if they returned among us, they would recognize in us the men they were during their lives and whom they would have wished to remain if they had escaped death.

Yes, France is faithful to the spirit of the French who fell during the Great War and of those Americans who fell by their sides on the blood-stained soil of our fatherland. France has not been an unworthy guardian of that sublime heritage. She has not forgotten the example that all those young men gave to the world. During twenty years she has consecrated all her efforts to the establishment of peace among men. She has consented to the greatest sacrifices for it. She has never pronounced a word, she has never accomplished an act, that was a word or act of menace or oppression. She can wait with serenity the judgment of history. And did not the eminent ambassador of the United States to France already anticipate that judgment last Sunday, when, at the commemorative ceremony for Joan of Arc, he said, "At this moment the most powerful allies of France are the eternal verities: the love the man of every country bears toward his home, his fatherland, his liberty." And only a few minutes ago, M. Bernard Ragner, commander for France of the American Legion, in his turn has offered us the same moving testimony.

If we could arrange conversations among the peasants of our countryside and the farmers of your great prairies, the workers of our factories and the laborers in your industrial cities, our doctors, our lawyers, our engineers, our businessmen and yours, they would soon make the discovery that they think in the same manner, in spite of the distance which separates them and in spite of the differences that exist between their languages, their races and their customs.

Frenchmen desire nothing but their own happiness. They wish to live in friendship with all men. They do not think of looking beyond their frontiers, unless it be to seek among other peoples examples of activity, of energy and of reasonableness. They wish to collaborate with those others for the ultimate good of humanity. They have never had the pretention of presenting themselves as a predestined race, superior to all others and fit to enslave those others. Their greatest happiness, on the contrary, consists in feeling themselves like the noblest and most peaceful among others.

Such is France. She is animated only by the desire for

collaboration. From the humblest of her sons to those who have charge of directing her, a single spirit presides over all her enterprises. She plays no double game on the map of the world. When she proposes peace, it is to peace that she sincerely consecrates her efforts. Her government does nothing but express the will of the people. She is a free nation, a democracy like yours. She is clearly responsible for her own destiny.

But, like all free nations, she cannot allow those things which seem to her more precious than life itself to be placed in danger. She is the homeland of human dignity, but also the country of courage and heroism.

This is why any attempt at hegemony or domination will find her determined to defend with her liberty the liberty of the world. She will be found always living up to herself, strongly united and resolute before peril.

But in spite of renewed threats, in spite of the uncertainties of the present hour, this France does not wish to abandon the hope of saving peace. She consecrates herself entirely to that labor, for months to come, in a magnificent calm, with a will beyond enfeeblement.

Thanks to the union of all her sons, thanks to a voluntary discipline, she has brought her production to its greatest intensity and has formidably increased her means of defense. For weeks she has asked her young soldiers to mount vigilant guard on the frontiers beyond which rise menacing clouds. She is making every effort to join her action to the action of all the peoples that wish peace with honor. She hopes that these efforts will suffice to prevent the world from being plunged into catastrophe. She will hold on as long as necessary, uninfluenced by lassitude or fear.

This is what France has done with the heritage of your dead. She had not forgotten the lesson of humanity and of courage they gave to the world. She has not permitted their example to be proscribed. She has thought that fidelity to heroes does not consist merely in watching over their tombs, but in maintaining with energy, in all its nobility, the ideal which seemed to them more important than life itself.

A Memorial Day speech, delivered May 28, 1939.

THE URGE TO ACTION

CONFERRING OF SPECIAL POWERS

Gentlemen, as the Minister of Finance has explained
to you, it is obviously in the financial repercussions of
the international crisis that we must seek the origin of
the bill now before you.

I think it will be enough for me to tell you, without
quoting an abundance of figures, that but for this international crisis the government, as pledged to Parliament,
would have kept all its engagements on the financial side.

I had declared that the new minimum financial basis
I had then set, and which would bring sterling to a rate
of about 179, would not descend any further. I notice
tonight that, in spite of so many weeks of grave anxiety,
this rate has not dropped.

I said that, contrary to many predictions, we could
hope for an important return of capital. It will be enough
to bring to your notice that a capital of nearly nineteen
billions of francs has come back to the country since my
government has been in office. I will add, so as to leave

no doubt, that this government is perhaps the only one, or in any case one of the few, which, for a long time, has never had recourse to loans from the Bank of France.

I believe these to be statements of facts that no one here will think of challenging.

But, as the Minister of Finance has proved with precise figures, in following facts, so to speak, day by day, this crisis has thrown public finances into the difficulty which he himself has brought to your attention.

We shall have to face these financial consequences. As the Finance Minister stated, we cannot give approximate figures, for the very simple reason that our troops are not yet demobilized.

It is the essential reason. For this same reason, we cannot give you tonight the full details of our plan.

I will add that after the spectacle of the dramatic financial events of the previous days, we have to observe a caution and measure in the words we use which all those who have once had to assume a like responsibility will not fail to understand.

I do not wish to use stratagems. I want, even less, to play some political game which I would think unworthy of the present situation, unworthy also of the very position which I now occupy.

Conferring Of Special Powers

The situation is too grave to allow words that are anything but clear and precise. I declare here, what I have already declared to a great number of members of this Assembly, whatever their party, who have asked me questions: I am appealing, in this hour, to all Frenchmen to exercise their will; what I am demanding from France is the whole of her driving power.

It is in this spirit that I am asking you to vote for this bill, without which it would be impossible for me to fulfill for another hour the task I have set myself.

I have already told the Committee of Ways and Means that I was supposed to control of the exchange market. Without a doubt some may be of a different opinion. In certain discussions some members have eloquently pleaded the cause of this system. I am its resolute adversary because its first consequence would be to precipitate a mass exportation of capital.

As control of the exchange market would demand, from the technical point of view, days and even weeks of adjustment—as it has in dictator countries where it has been used—the result would be an extremely swift and harmful flight of capital, a real drainage of the country's resources.

The second reason of my opposition is that I do not

want two French currencies: one at home, the other abroad.

My third reason is that France is a country which is largely an importer of raw materials, with an economic situation very different from that of Germany or Russia, who have organized this control, and that from my point of view it would be absolute ruin for France to be submitted to this dual financial regime.

I will add that it is not by chance that, in totalitarian countries where this control is the basis of the regime, or in any case its financial aspect, the working classes too often have to bear the cost of the operation. For, in order to avoid importations, destructive of the home currency, these classes have to submit to particularly hard conditions of existence, which, I think, would not be accepted by the workers of our country.

I will not press the matter any further. But I do want publicly to renew the declarations I have already made, either to the Committee of Ways and Means or to different political groups of the Assembly who have asked me questions.

In the same way I am hostile to the forced conversion of government stocks, and I admit that I cannot understand how we could proceed with this forceful and arbitrary operation against men to whom all governments have appealed, in times of crisis, to save the finances of their country.

It is evident that we have to reorganize the whole of our economic system. It is evident that we must put into operation an extensive reform involving the very structure of the budget. It is also evident, as several speakers have pointed out, that the revaluation of the gold stock which has been mentioned here and at the Committee of Ways and Means may be, tomorrow, one of the tasks of the government.

What you must ask the government, even more than the reason for the delay of its plan, is the spirit in which it intends to act during the few weeks it will be granted the special powers that are the object of this bill.

It is this spirit that actuated the declaration I made here this afternoon. I ended up by telling you that there was not an hour to lose, that we had to call for all the French driving power without which the country will not be able to face the critical events that, I feel, may be nearer than any of us think.

Peace, as I have told you here, will have to be won day by day.

This means that all Frenchmen, whatever their status

or class, must make whatever effort, even consent to whatever sacrifice, may be necessary to save the country.

Think of it! More than a million men were ready, if the safety of the country had demanded it, to shed their blood, even sacrifice their lives; how could we, then, conceive that there might be any Frenchmen with so little sense of their duty toward their fatherland as to refuse the indispensable effort that we are asking of them?

I have been told—and, strange to say, the point has been stressed: we do recognize the necessity of increasing production.

It is clear that the real means of bringing a remedy to our impoverished finances is to increase national revenue; I have said so in many speeches, I do not retract anything I have said on the subject in the past.

Do you really think it necessary, gentlemen, for me to develop this at length?

I have always said that sacrifices were not to be asked from only one category of citizens; I have also asserted that, having myself voted for the labor legislation, as most members of the two Houses have done, I had never had any intention of wielding the weapon that would destroy it. I have formed, on the contrary, the firm resolve to maintain it, but this can only be done by work and toil.

Conferring Of Special Powers

On the other hand, following various incidents that are still fresh in every memory, I have expressed my views about this social legislation to parliamentary delegations and to my own party; what I then expressed to my political friends still remains my way of thinking.

I, too, want to make an appeal to the working class. I, too, want to appeal, with all my strength, to its conscience, and I have no other desire than to obtain its cooperation in the necessary labor increase to the national output. I shall demand it over and over again from the working class: I shall ask it as a man who has a right to say here, as much as anyone, that he is a son of the people, that he loves the people and knows them, and that his desire is to see the constant improvement of the standard of living of the workers, in so far as it is possible.

Lastly, I have been asked, in various ways, about the question of control of these decrees which will result from the conferring of special powers.

We can, of course, conceive several means of control. But I have myself proposed that the chairmen and general reporters in the finance committees of the two assemblies be consulted by the government, in order that the decrees which are made be well adapted to the purpose of the law upon which you have just voted.

In Defense Of France

It goes without saying that if it is necessary to elaborate the discussion, I am ready to do so. It is not at all my intention to forge a party instrument. It is a work of public salvation which I want to undertake solely in the interest of the country, and it is to this end that I am asking you to collaborate with the government and to give us your confidence.

Gentlemen, my appeal is addressed to the whole Assembly, to the whole country. You will excuse me if I say that those who perhaps have the greatest interest in hearing it are those who are most attached to the parliamentary form of government, to the republican regime itself.

Indeed, you have had the example of neighboring democracies who sank into financial disorder till the day a dictator appeared. The French Revolution was not in reality defeated by European armies, but by the "assignats," sound or unsound, that, by degrees, caused the rising of the whole of the country people and even the working people of the cities against the revolutionary power.

It is not by apathy and the taste for an easy life that you will defend, against all the dangers that surround them, the parliamentary form of government, the Re-

Conferring Of Special Powers

public and democracy, which our forefathers founded and which are our inheritance, but by your virile resolution, your courage, your will to take the responsibilities, to guide the people instead of following them. The people of this country will be saved, in fact, only by their own voluntary effort, if they want to keep their political and social liberties.

Such are, gentlemen, the very simple and very frank words I had to address to you. I do not know if I have succeeded in converting or convincing anyone. But for many days and many nights I have fought to save the threatened peace. I have fought to try to make this peace less bitter, hard and cruel to a friendly people, indeed for many days and nights I have led this hard fight.

I will spend, if it is necessary, other days and nights for this new fight for financial recovery, because it is, in my opinion, if we win it, the very condition of the safeguarding of our liberty.

Speech delivered in the Chamber of Deputies, October 4, 1938, during the discussion of the bill conferring special powers.

FOREIGN, ECONOMIC AND HOME POLICY OF THE GOVERNMENT

My dear Friends,[1]

I am happy—is there any need to tell you?—to find myself once more among you. In the hard fights we have to lead, it is a comfort to find oneself among men who have given so many proofs of their devotion to the Republic and the country. To all those who chose you as their representatives at this vast congress, to all of you who are gathered here, I address my most cordial and grateful greeting.

You will easily realize that, at the present time, it is no longer possible for the head of the government to address himself only to his party. It is to the whole of France that it befits him to speak. Moreover, it is to the credit of the Radical party that they have not had to make any effort to recognize the identity of their own interests with those of the nation itself.

When we examine the present situation in Europe and throughout the world, what is the prevailing fact, what is the element that surpasses all others in importance

[1]*The Radical Socialist Congress at Marseilles.*

and scope? It is that peace, which seemed lost, has been saved, and it is that in peace we have to solve all our problems.

There is no need to recall that, during the last weeks we have just lived through, this peace has been threatened by many perils. There is no need to retrace for you an outline of this European crisis that led us very near catastrophe. There is no need to tell you at the price of what efforts and hard sacrifices we were able at last to settle this crisis.

What I want to stress once again before you, with all the strength I possess, is that for the whole of European civilization, for our ideal of liberty, for our country, for Czechoslovakia itself, the present situation resulting from the Munich Agreement is still preferable to that which would exist if we had not avoided war.

I have explained in Parliament that I understood perfectly, because I lived it myself, the inner drama which was enacted in each French conscience during this crisis. But today I cannot countenance talk of capitulation on the part of France. I know and I measure the consequences of this agreement; but I know that we did not yield to coercion and that if, at Munich, I had found myself confronted with an ultimatum, if I had not been able to make my voice heard and to discuss on an equal footing, I would have come back to Paris and I would have called the nation to resistance. The action taken at Munich has been a reasonable one.

I find it hard to understand, unless I understand it too well, a kind of campaign that is being started against an agreement which, on the very night of its signature, obtained the approval of men and women in all countries who would have had to pay with their blood or their tears the recourse to brutal force. Since I try to say only sensible things, and since, unmoved by acclamations or invectives, I think only of the lasting interest of the country, I feel indignant to see some men who consider these events as a subject for political controversies.

After all, am I not entitled to say that, at the time when perils were accumulating and the terrible event of a war seemed to be only a question of hours or of minutes, some who had been and who have again become adamant, ready to go as far as war, were at that time showing only a faltering resolution, to say the least? I would allow criticisms only from those who could remind me that, in those tragic hours, they came forward to tell me to go to war rather than accept any compromise. I will allow criticisms only from those who did not feel relieved at the announcement of my departure for Munich. What is all this hypocrisy, that consists of striking attitudes and giving lessons when danger is past, and remaining silent and trembling at the very moment when it is necessary to be resolute to the end?

No doubt, one party can tell me that they have always been advocating intransigence, though war might ensue, and that they have disapproved of negotiation. It is the Communist party who, on the other hand, have demonstrated their total opposition by their vote in Parliament and by their daily recriminations throughout the country.

The violence and intransigence of this party have paralyzed my course of action. When their papers and speakers were vulgarly attacking Mr Neville Chamberlain, who has worked with admirable faith to save peace, did they not then weaken France's position? When they were every day sending requests and ultimatums to the French government, did they facilitate our task? When they cast aspersions upon the governments with whom we were engaged in perilous negotiations, did they not risk hindering all chances of agreement and so plunging us into war? When they maintain now that the partial mobilization we had to order was only a screen for our surrender, they willfully slander us, because if, one day, this were believed by the misguided masses, it might render impossible, in another emergency, the resort to the same measure which, I repeat, has greatly contributed to save peace.

We are not fooled by the charges of the Communist leaders. While all Frenchmen have courageously answered the call of the country, while they deserve all the gratitude of the nation, I am bound to say that, in another sphere, the political attitude of the leaders of the Communist party has resulted, not in any support, but in a sabotage of the work of the government. I am forced to say the same about those others who, knowingly, have tried during these critical weeks to undermine the morale of the nation, but who broke themselves on the rock of national dignity.

When one wishes a government to say peace and honor, one does not publicly challenge its possibilities of action; one does not assert, against all truth, that the country is incapable of resistance; nor does one question the leaders of national defense.

We have maintained peace and the dignity of France.

We are resolved to persevere.

Our policy will be based on the fundamental interest of our country and will be adapted to the structure of the new situation.

Foreign, Economic And Home Policy

The fundamental interest of France is the safeguarding of her security. But French security is not solely limited to our continental frontiers. It is, on the contrary, conditioned by the freedom of the communications maintained between the Metropolis and its Empire.

From this city of Marseilles, which is not the land's end of France but the very heart of the French Empire, a sort of living link between metropolis and colonies, I want to emphasize the fact that France is an Empire. Beyond its continental frontiers is a vast zone of security as precious as the metropolis itself. That is where lies, in large part, the future of France. We consider this as intangible.

Does this mean that this Empire will be the only basis of our policy, of our national grandeur? Such is not our intention. The radiance of France will always go beyond our most remote frontiers.

France will be present everywhere. Everywhere she will unite her efforts to those which may be made in the interests of justice and peace. As I declared before Parliament, she will try to add new and renewed friendships to existing ones. She will bring complete good will to the examination of all problems. She thinks that, where everyone wants to be prudent and fair, peaceful settlements can be obtained wherever there is litigation. Whether it be in her relations with Germany or with Italy, she is convinced that if, on either side, the only preoccupation is the defense of national interests, agreements can intervene that will bring the most useful contribution to the strengthening of peace. This is equally true concerning the amicable relations that tie France to the friendly nations of eastern Europe.

Thus, the basis of French diplomacy rests, above all, on close co-operation with Great Britain—freely chosen co-operation, founded on a common ideal and common interests, co-operation in mutual respect and equality. This co-operation does not exclude any other. We are open to all possible ententes. When, at Munich, I felt the heart of the German people, I could not help thinking, as I had done at Verdun at the height of the war, that between the French and the German peoples, in spite of all difficulties, there are strong reasons for mutual esteem which must lead to loyal collaboration.

I have always firmly desired this collaboration. Whatever the differences in their forms of government, the two nations which so often confronted each other on the battlefield must understand that in modern times war is never a solution and that it is possible to solve all questions by the loyal entente of all peoples.

Foreign, Economic And Home Policy

Such is the method that must allow us to maintain peace. To this peace we have made sacrifices. But we do not want it to be distorted and presented as the first halt on the road that would lead to abdication. Did we not have to solve a crisis that had lasted for twenty years? And I have the right to say that during those twenty years I have not ceased, with my friends, to demand for a prompt solution of the unsettled state of Europe. It would have been easier and less costly some years ago. But there is no room for sterile regrets if this saved peace marks for France the end of her past errors and the beginning of a new era.

Such a decision can be valid only if it rests on the strength of the nation—if, once taken by the government, it is ratified by the whole people and if, to the great hope then awakened in all hearts, there comes immediately the response of a common effort for work and respect for the laws of the Republic.

No sooner are we freed from the menace of war than we are assailed by formidable difficulties in our financial and economic life.

Do you know what would be the total of the ordinary budget of 1939? Sixty-four billions. That of the extraordinary budget, thirty billions. If you add to these figures the provision for the sinking fund, you arrive at the total of 102 billions of francs of financial charges.

One hundred and two billions of francs in 1939!

To meet these charges, on what receipts can we count? On about sixty-six billions.

The total amount of Treasury charges for 1939 would be fifty-three billions if we did not act.

An expenditure of 102 billions! And that for a national income of 220 billions of francs.

I am asking: can this situation last any longer? Can the national income be swallowed up in this way? Is not the disproportion overwhelming for French currency? If it were allowed to go on, France would rush headlong into bankruptcy.

We refuse to allow our country to involve itself any longer in a situation which will end with the foundering of liberty, its republican form of government and perhaps its very independence and integrity.

We shall have to set our finances in order, to reduce Treasury charges, to make a vigorous effort towards balancing the budget. But all these efforts can bear fruit only if we maintain at the same time order and peace at home and abroad, together with a certain political stability. Experience has shown that it is the indispensable condition of the recovery of public finances.

In fact, for us, the most imperative necessity is the increase of national income, hence the increase of production and exchanges, hence the increase of effort on the part of all Frenchmen, employers and workmen.

I had only to issue, in the course of this summer, a call to work to let loose against me attacks and insults of an unheard-of violence.

Did the authors of these attacks and insults want me to remain silent, passive, to allow France to lose her strength every day until the crash? I came to office as a free man. I have studied the situation. I have arrived at the conclusion that the initial cause of the crisis that undermines our country is the weakening of our production. In Germany, from 1929 to 1937, production has increased by 17 per cent; in England by 24 per cent; in the Scandinavian countries, by 30 to 50 per cent. In France, national production in the same period has decreased by 25 per cent. I only did my duty as a Frenchman when I said that this situation could not last.

If France goes to ruin, she will be the prey of civil discords. To try to maintain liberty, is that to betray the working class?

In Defense Of France

If France goes to ruin, she will be attacked. To want to preserve peace, is that to betray the working class?

If France goes to ruin, she is vanquished. To want to oppose servitude for us all, is that to betray the working class?

When one says that France must recover, does that make one the agent of national and international capitalism, a traitor to the working class—is that to speak the language of the fascists?

There again, the Communist party risk, by their violence, driving the country to a dramatic destiny.

What is this absurd legend that they would like to make the country believe that the call to work arises from the fascist ideology? What is the object of this crusade directed against the government, but from which France will inevitably suffer? In towns as in villages, outside and inside factories, workers are enticed to resist governmental initiative. We say that there is no national duty more imperative than to increase and improve national production.

We hear: "France must be strong, she must be in a position to impose her will—if necessary by her armed force." And the same voices call out: "Do not work more than forty hours, refuse to manufacture airplanes for more than forty hours a week! Regard as traitors those who ask you to work extra hours in accordance with economic necessity."

When I ask for a vigorous effort, I ask it from all Frenchmen and not only from the working class. I will not tolerate a reactionary policy whose effect would be to reduce the comfort of workers and interfere with their freedom. And I know that we must see to it that in many industries the tools as well as the methods of work are changed for the better. Concern for the common good must be the preoccupation of all.

Paid holidays, the right to strike counterbalanced by the right to work, the application of the procedure of arbitration and the right to appeal from that arbitration to a referee outside the dispute, the fight against unemployment by occupational classification, and the reabsorption of unemployed men who can be turned into useful workers—all these are measures which can really improve the lot of the working class. They are measures which really help to increase human dignity.

I am myself the son of a workingman. I am entitled to speak of these questions, not theoretically, but as a man who has, for years, discussed them when seated with his own people at the family table.

In Defense Of France

I understand that workmen must have felt an immense
joy on the day they acquired the right to fresh air,
to relaxation in the mountains or by the sea. It was
monstrous that the workers in great cities in particular
should have been unable to enjoy the rest that allows
man to feel a new vigor. It is also normal for these
workers to have some relaxation every week. To organize
all these rights was simply to acknowledge the dignity
of the human person. But to ask these same workers
for a few extra hours of work with a simultaneous increase in salary at a time when this work especially
permits us to surmount the perils that threaten us, is
that to interfere with human dignity? I cannot believe
it. I am sure this is not a natural sentiment of French
workers. Not one of those I have known would have
taken that view.

I am asking workmen to think over what I have just
said. Do they really believe that this battle into which
some want to drag them is a fight for their real interests?
What can that bring to their homes, their wives, their
children? In struggling for paid holidays and arbitration,
the workers were fighting for their dignity, for their
right to the life of a free and proud man. To achieve
this result, they have had the support of all democrats,

all republicans. But by refusing the country the work necessary to its defense, they would only bring about disorder and bankruptcy and set up against them the whole forces of the nation.

It is not at all our intention to abrogate the forty-hour law, though it is not in force in any other great country. But it is imperative to adapt it without any idle formalities, wherever required, to the real needs of industry and commerce and the exigencies of economic life. I hope that this adjustment, the necessity of which no one seriously questions, will soon be effected in an atmosphere of mutual confidence and social peace. Social legislation is of value only if provision is made for sanctions. The employer who evades the law must be punished in the same way as the worker. The last word must remain with the law. The supreme authority of the State must not be flouted.

We have made provision in this legislation for a procedure of arbitration with a right of appeal to a third party. Of what use is this if the parties can refuse with impunity to accept the final decisions that do not give them satisfaction? We shall take all necessary measures to see that these decisions are respected.

We have recognized the rights of trade unions, but

in the very interest of workmen we cannot permit their delegates to be foreigners or men with bad police records.

We have recognized the right to strike, but there again, in the interest of a movement of protest which is often well founded, we say that the strike cannot be the result of the sudden decision of a few men, but that it must be decided by a free and secret ballot.

This is our way of thinking and it is the programme that we shall accomplish in the near future.

The government feels that it has done its best, both for the working class and for national production. We shall persevere with this plan, whatever organized attacks there may be.

In order to introduce these necessary reforms, we must first obtain a recovery of the public spirit. French consciences are the prey of too much propaganda, too many theories which, deceptively clad, too often hide foreign interests or ambitions. We are a free country; anyone in France has a right to say what he thinks and to defend what seems to him to be the truth. But we do not want to become the lists of all the contradictions and controversies that tear the modern world.

We will not permit foreign forces, whatever their origin and inspiration, to interfere with our national life or to claim the right to show us, Frenchmen, what the interest and duty of France are. We will not allow Frenchmen to become the agents of this propaganda in our country. We will still less permit foreigners to wrench from us the right of control and decision that must be reserved only for the French. France remains a haven of refuge, but I declare that if she intends to remain hospitable, she will insist upon respect for the fundamental law of hospitality, which is, not to intervene in the affairs of your host. Those who would not comply with this law would place themselves outside the bounds of French hospitality.

Hitlerian Germany, Fascist Italy, Communist Russia all forbid democratic propaganda in their respective territories. It is their right as sovereign states. The French Republic, which may perhaps have been too patient, will be on the lookout to make impossible any enterprise that does not have its roots in the real interests of the nation.

Citizens, the government means to defend the republican regime in all its spheres of action. France is and will always be the land of the rights of man. All her children, without any distinction of origin or creed, are equal before the law.

In Defense Of France

We want a strong Republic, a vigorous democracy, capable of resisting all attacks that could be directed against her. We have nothing to fear from our adversaries. If, by chance, there was one day an attempt of force against the Republic, citizens, army, the whole power of the nation would rise to break it. But daily intrigues, frequent governmental crises without any real cause, the uncertainty that governmental instability creates in the life of the nation, might all provoke one day the skepticism or the weariness of the public spirit. What must be feared in France—as has happened in other countries—is that the failure of the legislative power or the inertia of the executive power would make the people indifferent to our regime of liberty.

Citizens, the effort that is to enable us to face the difficulties of our time, the immense effort that is to transform our life within the nation, later to make it radiate beyond our frontiers—such an effort cannot be the result of a miracle. There cannot be a miracle where the recovery of France is concerned. We do not need either a savior or a man of destiny; we need determined workers who, day after day, perform their task and prepare the task of the morrow.

The miracle will come, but it will be the result of

labor and patience. The country will be saved, but it will not owe its safety to the sudden appearance of a savior; the country will be saved of its own accord by the joint effort of all its sons. All the great events in the course of history that we have been able to call French miracles have happened in this way. The Battle of the Marne, it has been said, was a miracle. But it was prepared by the vision of our High Command, and it was made possible by the sacrifice of hundreds of thousands of men whose courage had not failed after days and nights of reverses.

When this government took office, we said in the ministerial statement: "A great free country can be saved only by its own efforts."

Our greatest force, within and without our frontiers, is the force of liberty. Everything is possible for Frenchmen because the French are free men. Who is the one among them who would dare refuse the country either his work, or his money, or his blood, since he knows that in the disorders of the present world this country has known the way to preserve everything that makes the life of man worth living? It is in the name of liberty that we are entitled to ask of every Frenchman the sacrifice that these critical times have made necessary.

In Defense Of France

France is a nation of peasants who know the natural delays of all man's works. They know that for the harvest to come, they must have plowed and sowed. Let us plow today. Let us sow tomorrow. Let us protect our fields against the vicissitudes of the seasons, against the ravages of the tempest.

Soon, harvest will come.

Speech delivered at the Radical Socialist Congress at Marseilles, October 27, 1938.

SALUTE TO THE VETERANS OF
THE GREAT WAR

As PRIME MINISTER of the government of the Republic and as a soldier in the Great War, I address the grateful salute of the country to the veterans of France and our colonial Empire, whose representatives are gathered here, without any distinction of class or creed.

To the veterans of the Allied countries, I want to express the faithfulness of our brotherly affection. France does not distinguish between them and her own sons. They know that their place is reserved among us at all our gatherings for the commemoration of events over which we mourn or rejoice.

Twenty years ago, my dear comrades, war had just ended. During fifty-one months, on French soil from the Yser to the Vosges or farther afield with expeditionary forces, we were brought face to face with it. We had learned all its secrets: terrible secrets for which we had paid with our sufferings or our blood; for which many thousands of our comrades had paid with their lives. We had had one of the most frightful of human

[127]

experiences. We knew the meaning of war as nobody before us had known it.

And now, twenty years later, we realize that we are only beginning to learn what real peace is. Through a new threat of war, we came to this realization. For many years we have perhaps had the illusion that we had paid the price of peace in the trenches of Flanders, Champagne, Verdun and Argonne. But we know now that peace is never permanently secured and that it shuns those who would only enjoy its benefits and would not consent to fight for it.

For the peace we want cannot be simply a refusal of risk. It would not be insured by the sole fact that we would refuse to go to war. It needs to be supported by a virile resolution. It lays claim to as many moral forces as war itself, for it can only be peace with honor and liberty.

The moral strength of France is, then, the main condition of peace. Only moral energy can enable us to speak to other peoples on an equal footing and to obtain a hearing from them. To let this strength expand freely, radiate with all its power, we must first give back to the country the sense of some fundamental truths.

Veterans of the Great War, you have never allowed

these truths to be forgotten. You know that the essential truth, the one that is the condition of all others, is that service of country must come first. You know that such a conception of duty renders impossible civil discord and hatred between the sons of the same country. Those who are united by the same will to serve the country cannot be set up against one another. There can only be between them feelings of brotherhood and love. I know that you understand the necessity for this tightening of French unity: the fellowship of arms which binds you all is the highest expression of this union of hearts. You can be, in this great task, the leaders of the country.

But to be able to build a real peace, this moral power of France must be supported and maintained by a creative impetus, a force of production that she is still far from possessing at the moment.

All that I have said would only be vain phrases if our labor were not to correspond to our will for peace and our love of country.

I find again here, recurring with implacable logic, the theme I have bent all my efforts to develop ever since I have had the honor to be Prime Minister. I am not sure that I have always been completely understood. All the more reason for my insisting upon and for giving once more the rule in which I believe and which we must apply for our safety.

To maintain peace, to insure the security of France and be in a position to ward off any attempts that might be directed against her, we must be strong, morally and materially: and the source of strength, for a great nation like ours, is work.

I have said it, repeated it, I will repeat it indefatigably: our output is not what it ought to be. While the production of peoples around us has shown, in recent years, a considerable increase, ours has, on the contrary, shown a decrease. This statement is not—alas!—an unreliable one. All French people ought to know and repeat ceaselessly to themselves that, from 1929 to 1937, national production increased by 17 per cent in Germany; by 24 per cent in England; by 30 to 50 per cent in the Scandinavian countries—while during the same period in France it has decreased by 25 per cent. Such a situation could not last without endangering the independence and the very existence of the nation.

The strength of a country is only the result of its capacity for production and creation. The burdens of national defense are all the heavier if they are not counterbalanced by a production superior to what is

directly required for this defense. A weak man, clad in
armor, will find it heavier than an athlete would. We
must not let France be crushed by the armor she is
compelled to wear.

Everything is connected in the life of a great country.
Production, Treasury, currency, birth rate, even morals,
are in close relationship. None of these factors of national
life and strength can disappear without dragging with
it all the other elements of life.

You know the difficulties of our finances and of our
economic life. A nation cannot remain great and strong
if it resigns itself to the growing deficit of its budgets,
the permanent resort to inflation, and a system of government loans bearing interest at an ever-increasing rate.

The time has come when everyone must understand
that, before long, he will greatly imperil both himself
and his possessions unless he resolutely devotes himself
to the public safety. We appeal to all classes, to all
Frenchmen. Everyone must collaborate for the recovery
of the country, according to his resources and his capa-
bilities. It is under this condition only that we shall be
able to secure the stability of our currency, without
which we would rapidly approach the catastrophe of the
"assignats." It is under this condition only that we shall

again find prosperity and that we shall be able to look forward to new and fertile prospects.

When making this appeal to labor, I ought to be understood by all French people, for it is intended for them all, employers and workmen, intellectual workers as well as peasants. It is with the interest and future of all that I am concerned. When I say that France must go back to work, I tell workmen that they must produce more, and I will keep on repeating it to them. But I also tell employers that they must show more initiative and boldness, that they must, above all, stop seeking immediate benefit or the illusion of security, and think of the common interest first. Everyone must give the country what he has to give: work, money or intelligence.

I know what ideal spurs on the veterans of the Great War. I was guided by their spirit when I chose the road to fruitful effort and not that to ruinous ease. Tomorrow, all Frenchmen will have to face reality. Tomorrow, we shall accomplish what we consider as a sacred duty towards the country. Tomorrow, we shall say to all: the time has come to choose between the slow decay of the country and its recovery by virtue of effort. The government—and I want to pay all my colleagues and particularly my friend M. Paul Reynaud, Finance Minister, the homage their courage and labor deserve—the government asks from all, will exact from all if needs be, the sacrifices and discipline that are necessary.

There is, moreover, no question of asking the French to renounce those things that make up the joy and dignity of their life. It is only a question of asking them to break away from a certain indolence, a certain ease. It is only a question of asking them for the effort that free and proud men must always be able to give.

Can there be a greater misfortune than to feel one's country lose every year some of its strength, of its substance, and see it slowly advance toward a miserable destiny? Is there a greater trial than to feel one's destiny bound to that of a great country which risks becoming a secondary and subordinate nation, left only with the prestige and grandeur of its past, because of the decline of its birth rate, the slowing of its production, the embarrassment of its finances, the fall of its currency?

I think, on the contrary, that the French would be happier than they are today if tomorrow, working more, striving more, they could find round the family table a greater number of children than they have today, secure in the knowledge that the future of those children is assured.

When a people really recovers, its factories begin to hum everywhere, its finances are healthy, its currency is strong, the work of its artists, scientists and writers radiates over the world, its children fill schools and everyone feels more joyous, contented and free.

When it is a question of offering one's life, I count upon you who, during the four years of war, showed the country what can be accomplished by a spirit of sacrifice and discipline. I count upon you to show this same spirit when it is a question of permitting a great nation, whose destiny is identified with some of the greatest human hopes, to continue to live as one of the great powers of the world.

Veterans of the Great War, I have not wanted you to be the objects of a decree. It is not to the law, it is to your will that I have decided to appeal. You, too, must make sacrifices, but I am convinced that you will consent to them willingly. Without these sacrifices the nation would cease to be solvent for the debt incurred to you. A ruined country cannot even pay the sacred debt of gratitude. I have placed my confidence in you. When I appeal to the spirit of veterans, I address myself to what is best in the country. As, twenty years ago, you led your colors to victory, you will know today how to be the resolute leaders of the French nation. You will work with us with one heart, so that France

Salute To The Veterans Of The Great War
will find again, through the effort of her sons, the grandeur that always was hers.

If there are some in your country who find the task too heavy, if there are some who do not gladly give what is demanded of them, tell them that, day after day, night after night, exhausted but resolute, shaken by all terrors, you bore for four years sufferings that imagination cannot conceive. Tell them that the tasks of today are only light, compared with what you had to endure during the great turmoil. Tell them to think of what their existence would be, on this very day, if, in this autumn of 1938, we had to advance again along the bloody road of 1914.

You will tell them, with the authority that your experience gives you: "Do not complain. It would be shameful to complain. For we have seen men ready to die because they knew that their death was serving France. Have the strength to live for her and do not refuse her your work, where others offered her the last sacrifice."

Speech delivered, November 12, 1938, at the banquet of the Veterans of the Great War.

[135]

FINANCIAL RECOVERY

You know the financial situation. The balance sheet expected by the country has been published. Figures, statistics, speak more clearly than words. Arguments are useless in face of facts that direct all to a common resolve: we must find a way out; we must straighten up the financial situation of France.

Is there a single Frenchman, is there a single Frenchwoman, who supposes that public charges may be more than half the national income and that France may spend about one hundred and thirty-seven billions in a year, while her resources are not more than eighty-five billions?

Is there a single Frenchman or a single Frenchwoman who does not deduce from this that a vigorous effort is indispensable, and that they must take their share in it with all their energy and patriotic faith?

During these last weeks, I was not spared advice.

People kept on repeating to me: "What are you waiting for? The situation is grave. The country is with you. It is aware of dangers ahead. It is ready for all sacrifices.

Financial Recovery

Not a single Frenchman would refuse, at this time, to bring his contribution to the common cause. Strike hard! Nobody will complain. But act quickly—and do not be afraid of using too heavy a hand."

It was in the midst of this chorus of encouragement that I assumed my responsibilities. On the 15th of November, recovery measures were published in the *Journal Officiel*.

You know these measures. They are severe. They correspond very exactly to the gravity of the situation. They call for sacrifices from all. They call for labor, capital and intelligence to co-operate for the safety of the country.

What is now taking place?

Advice and encouragement have turned into criticism. The very people who were urging me to dare all, to go with a heavy hand, to take a rapid decision, are now reproaching me for the measures we had to take. The same chorus with a full band is noisily performing around me. But while advice was given as a hummed accompaniment, criticism and reproaches involve loud crashes of the cymbals.

We are especially criticized because we introduced fiscal measures in the recovery plan. How could we have

acted otherwise? We may not have shown more imagination than our predecessors, but we showed no less, either.
Have there ever been recovery plans without fiscal
measures? Recovery plans without any such measures
are for the special use of the Opposition; but as soon as
this Opposition becomes Government, it has to comply
with the common rule. The resort to fiscal measures is
the price paid by those who hold office. To this day, all
schemes, either devised or brought into operation, have
contained them. And the supporters of the control of
the exchange markets themselves had to resort to fiscal
measures, though today they offer us their solution as
a miraculous one. Furthermore, may I add that the control of the exchange markets as a remedy to fiscal evasion
is a self-deception, since the capital now abroad would
remain outside our frontiers.

Our policy is to obtain the return of this capital. The
plan of my friend, M. Paul Reynaud, must bring about
this result: the mechanism which is to encourage these
returns has already been set to work. The very day
following the publication of the plan, more than a billion
francs came back to France.

Our aim is to obtain a reduction of the rate of interest
on loans that will develop the spirit of enterprise and

favor private initiative; to leave to everyone, within the limits of laws equitable for all, a maximum of freedom that will voluntarily be placed at the service of the nation.

The violence of the campaigns launched against our action proves that we are on the right road. If it were really believed that we had reached an impasse, should we be the object of so many virulent speeches, so many violent attacks? With smiling patience people would wait for our downfall. But, instead of rejoicing for the sake of the country, at the thought that success is possible our opponents are endeavoring to compromise it by spreading anxiety.

I denounce their malicious action. I do not care about the intrigues of which they are guilty. I will not yield to any of their maneuvers. I despise their threats. They will not succeed in breaking our will or in staying the impetus of France towards recovery. As for myself, I will no more be the man who would bring about bankruptcy than the man who would have brought war upon us.

All these campaigns run against the common sense of the country. I have the right to say that this common sense is unlikely to be upset as easily as some fancy.

In Defense Of France

However solitary a prime minister may be, immersed in the duties of his office, however aloof because of this very labor, the voice of the modest people of France reaches him all the same. You may rest assured that I pay great attention to all the evidence I collect. It is, moreover, a familiar voice. I know what courage, what good humor, what exact appreciation of things there are in the minds of these humble workers who are the strength of the nation. I know they are accepting the sacrifices demanded of them. I express here my gratitude to them in my own name and in that of the country.

My government is as deeply attached to the safety of the Republic and of liberty as it is to that of France herself. And that is why it will win.

I ask the French once more to observe what is happening beyond our frontiers. We are now living in the midst of a Europe set in motion, a Europe where powerful nations are bursting everywhere the old forms, a Europe where the law of effort, accelerated by discipline and even coercion, rules the lives of the peoples, a Europe where it would be vain for us, at the present time, to rely for our security on anything but our own strength.

While peoples, in this way, extend their power and

raise their vitality to the highest point, what do we French do? We live on our past; it has left us an admirable moral, intellectual and material inheritance. It has made a free man of every Frenchman.

But, if we content ourselves with living on our inheritance, if we limit ourselves to organizing our life in an easy way, if we refuse to make sacrifices for the common good and especially to submit to the vital law of effort, France then will take second rank among the nations. She will have no grandeur but that of her past. She will become a sort of museum, bearing witness to what has been and is no more. She will at the same time lose her independence and her comfort. She will wake from her stupor one day to find herself weak, ruined, and every Frenchman, dragged into the general collapse, will have to give up all hope of again becoming a free and happy man.

Listen to the friendly voices that come from abroad and encourage us to recover, wishing for the success of the experiment. Listen, also, to the hostile or envious voices that already proclaim our failure and gleefully prophesy political crises and disturbances.

Is not then the duty of the French clearly laid out for them? Let them think for a moment before they allow themselves to be dragged into polemics that can only injure the country.

What do the French want? What do you all want? The recovery of France and the maintenance of her liberty and peace.

The failure of our plan? How would it serve France's recovery? Do you think that our freedom, to which all workers are so justly attached, could then be maintained? Do you not think that the confusion and instability of which France would thus give a further example would secure an advantage for those who dream of imposing their domination upon the world?

The opponents as well as the supporters of the principles that actuate the decrees, even those who would have preferred the application of other doctrines, all must acknowledge a fact which compels recognition. It is that an experiment has begun, that it may succeed, that it is to the interest of all Frenchmen individually, of France as a whole, of all friends of peace, that it should succeed rapidly and in the most striking way.

Some learned articles have been written on the contagion of dictatorship. It is not by disorder that you will stop this contagion; it is by setting an example of discipline, it is by showing that democracy, with methods of freedom, can insure a proud and dignified life to a great nation.

Would not the union and discipline of France strengthen the friendship which binds us to Great Britain and tighten the bonds of sympathy which are so strong between France and the United States, while her weakness and her divisions would imperil them? And when I declare, in the name of the whole country, its will for peace with all peoples, its resolute attachment to the principles of the "rights of man," to racial equality, to the respect of the human person—do you not think that this necessary assertion will carry all the more weight if France shows herself nearer definite recovery, more confident in her future?

For my part, I have confidence in this recovery because I have confidence in the people of France. I have always kept my promises to them. I did not prophesy miracles; I told them that they would have to save themselves by virtue of their own endeavor. I told them that we would have to overcome immense difficulties and that we would do so by accepting heavy sacrifices.

I told them the truth yesterday. It is the truth that I tell them today. Here is the truth: the government will not be deterred by criticism or strangled by maneuvers;

it will pursue its action to the end with vigor and method. France is now on the way to recovery, nothing nor anyone will stop her.

Speech delivered at the banquet of the National Association of French Newspapers, November 17, 1938.

YESTERDAY AND TODAY

WHEN TAKING OFFICE, ten months ago, we said that national defense had to be considered as a whole. Both the events and our action have proved it. Once more I have to emphasize the fact that there has always been a direct relation between our internal disorders and our difficulties beyond the frontiers. On the other hand, once more I can state that everything that contributes to our internal recovery tends at the same time to enhance the prestige of France and to ward off the dangers that threaten her.

For ten months our government has been forced to fight simultaneously on two fronts. At the very outset it had to overcome lack of understanding, ill will, even, at times, dangerous conspiracies like the political general strike of November. At the same time it had to face serious problems abroad. Each time it found itself weakened or threatened by internal divisions, the peril from outside grew. Each time it had overcome disorder and brought back to the right path the misguided French energies, then it was, on the contrary, possible for the government to speak strongly in France's name.

Such a situation could not last indefinitely. Days to come are so charged with difficulties and cares that the government has the right to demand that the integrity of France and her Empire and the vital interests of the nation should have absolute priority over preoccupations of internal policy.

The policy of the government, you already know. It is both a policy of peace and a policy of national defense. The government does not want to take chances, but it does not want to abandon anything. It wants to spare French blood, but it is watchful of the interests of France. It will devote all its energy to prevent the outbreak of a conflict that would mark the end of Occidental civilization. But it will not allow the position and the interests of France to be imperiled, either by force or by cunning.

Events confirm only too well our previsions. Let them open all eyes! May the French understand that they belong to a privileged nation and that, whatever the sacrifices we ask from them, they have the benefit of a share of happiness that will be safeguarded only by a heroic resolution. Their first duty is to work. But work

Yesterday And Today

would not be of any value unless it could bear fruit in order and concord. Day by day French unity must be strengthened. On this condition only shall we be able to direct, without uncertainty, this foreign policy designed to save both peace and the grandeur of France.

Conclusion of the speech addressed, January 15, 1939, to the Executive Committee of the Radical Socialist party.

THE GUARD ON THE FRONTIERS

CORSICA

I

On my way to bring the greeting of the country to our Empire, I could not miss the opportunity of stopping here, because you are the land's end of France. It is from your island that I shall bring the salute of metropolitan France to France overseas. It is from this great port that our squadron will speed along these southern routes that have been for centuries, and become more and more every day, the routes of French initiative and valor. We shall bring with us a little of the air of the mother country—which is as well the air of your island. It was from your native shores that we wanted to convey the salute of France.

Do not think that the sea is a barrier between us. From Marseilles or from Toulon our squadrons and commercial lines trace between you and us routes easier and more rapid than some of the mountain roads that separate a number of French departments.

We are grateful to you for preserving your own

traditions and your own habits, for regional character strengthens the unity of France. Whatever our origin, we became French because we wanted to be French. France has not been made by mere chances of race, language or geography, but by the consent of men and a reasonable decision stronger and nobler than these chances.

France's genius is present everywhere. Far from weakening it, regional peculiarities only give it a stronger character. It is one and indivisible. Nowhere in the world in such a small area are human differences stronger, but nowhere, either, are the common ideal and hope more powerful. Nothing is more varied than France, but nothing has more unity than our country.

What makes us all French, even more than what we have received from France, is what we have given her. That is why each Frenchman finds himself reflected in her. Some find in her their tenacity and valiance; others their graciousness and cheerfulness; others their energy and eagerness; but everyone recognizes this atmosphere of civilization and humanity that makes us feel strongly united through a miraculous meeting of the accidents of history and the will of men.

How could you fail to find your own genius in the

genius of France, you Corsicans, since it was from this island that came, one day, a young man named Bonaparte, who was to become Napoleon? He was a soldier at the time the country's fate was to be decided on all her frontiers. Of a France attacked, he made a France victorious. Of a France buoyant with all enthusiasms and all hopes, he made a France organized and coherent. Revolutionary spirit found in him the man capable of stabilizing its conquests; and the will for order found in him the man capable of bringing to an end the convulsions of the country.

But it is not necessary to evoke here this exceptional man to show the ties that bind you to France. The unity of France and of the French has been achieved as much by the work of anonymous men who enabled her to live and were the humble makers of her grandeur as by the action of her kings, her emperors and her civil or military chiefs.

You, Corsicans, gave Bonaparte to France and she gave you back Napoleon. But you also gave her loyal servants, men of the land and men of the sea, peasants and sailors, soldiers and civil servants. Above all, you gave her your forty thousand dead in the Great War. Each of them, fisherman or shepherd, however humble he may have been, soldier of Craonne or Verdun, is a token of loyalty and love, of which the human value to the country is as great as the gift to her of the man of Austerlitz.

By the blood of our dead, the glory of our great men, the radiance of our culture, the joy and sweetness which characterize life in our country, by all the privileges of freedom and justice, France lives in each of us, and her reality cannot be doubted, nor can it be explained to those who do not want to understand her. Our community is founded as much on hopes as on memories. It is founded on the regard for human dignity, for the freedom of the individual and for the tutelary role of the State. There is no need for France to be aggressive and threatening. She is content with quiet assertion. She knows she is imperishable and indestructible because she lives first in the hearts and minds of men.

But this France, peaceful and quiet, this France who does not ever raise her voice, has a right to be sure of her strength. She is strong. I can say it to you who are soldiers and sailors. I can say it to you who know the meaning of service under the tricolor; to you who never spared your blood for her defense.

The squadron which takes us to Tunis will soon leave

Corsica

your roadstead. When you watch it bearing away from
your sight, recognize in it the force of the nation. Let
your fisherman go back to his boat and nets, your shepherd to his mountain and flock, your peasant to his
mattock and plow; let each of you go back to his trade,
his office, his work, with the serenity of those who know
they have nothing to fear but everything to expect from
the future.

*Speech delivered January 2, 1939, from the balcony of
Ajaccio Town Hall.*

CORSICA

II

Hᴏᴡ ᴄᴀɴ ɪ ᴇxᴘʀᴇss ᴛᴏ ʏᴏᴜ my grateful feelings and my emotion for the enthusiastic welcome you have given me today?

Indeed, in the life of a man whose work has been for so many years connected with the destiny of his country, there are often moving moments, difficult, sometimes tragic; but never, as today on this island, have I felt the heart of the country nearer to my heart.

A moment ago I was listening to the address of the mayor of Bastia. How happy I was to think he was heard at that very moment in France, in Europe, in the whole world. Despising boasts and threats, proud to belong to a country of reason and liberty, he proclaimed the undying attachment of Corsica to France and took the oath that you have all taken, as your sons will take after you, to fight and die if necessary.

To enable us all to take this oath, to enable us to keep it, whatever the uncertainties of the future, we must first have unity and understanding as between the sons of the same family.

As this morning in Ajaccio, all the representatives of Corsica, close to each other under the folds of the tricolor, wanted very much to accompany me. They are united here, in Bastia they will always be, because, as in the motto of Metz, the heroic city of Lorraine: "If you want peace without, you must have peace within, between you, citizens."

Ladies and gentlemen, I have to go, along the coast line of this beautiful island, to that section of northern Africa which is a part of France because it is perhaps the stronghold where rests the grandeur of the French Empire.

I shall bring it the salute of the whole French people, of all France's provinces, which became French more by a reasonable act of their own free will than by force, which never submitted to servitude, and which will remain free, because it is the destiny of France to prefer death to slavery.

Thank you again for your welcome. You did well, dear mayor and friend, to evoke some of these great Corsican figures—concerning whom the history of our country is sometimes a little too parsimonious—because in their lives one can appreciate the genius of your race, a race that will never bow down, but that gives itself freely in an enthusiasm of the heart.

Thank you again, my dear friends, for your welcome, which shall remain in my memory as long as I live; this welcome which today was heard everywhere and which bears witness to your loyalty towards our common mother country.

Again thank you. To end on a more familiar note, I am proud that in my sons' veins there is a little of this Corsican blood, because it is for me an assurance that, like you, they will always follow the path of courage and honor.

Speech delivered January 2, 1939, at the Bastia Theater in reply to the address of the mayor, M. de Montera.

TUNIS

I

Your Highness,

In the name of the whole French government, I bring to Your Highness the greeting of the protective nation.

The voyage I begin today in this beautiful land of Tunis is due to the solicitude of the government of the Republic for the Regency.

France and Tunis are indissolubly bound by the tie of treaties, and these ties are made stronger every day through reciprocal services and the growing prosperity that is their consequence. This solidarity manifests itself in all spheres, whether economic or intellectual, and thanks to this French and Tunisians every day learn to know each other better and to collaborate.

When the time came, Tunis answered the call to action and sacrifice. It has known how to practice self-restraint and collect itself in silence.

I assure Your Highness of France's readiness to contribute to the development of Tunisian riches and to give your country all the protection that might be needed.

In Defense Of France

This protection, she displayed in the past. The development of the economic wealth of Tunis, which is pursued methodically and to which we shall give all our attention, is a proof of that protection. France is prepared to give this protection in all quarters of the Empire, and Your Highness may rest assured that she will not at any time lose sight of the sacred duty which it is her historical mission to fulfill and to which her genius points.

France knows she can count upon the friendly and complete collaboration of the Tunisian people.

Address to the Bey of Tunis, January 4, 1939, in the Throne Room of the Palace of the Bardo.

TUNIS

II

THE RENEWED DECLARATIONS of attachment and loyalty which during the last months have been made to the mother country by the officials and populations of Tunis, Algeria and Morocco could not have remained unanswered.

As head of the government of the Republic, I have insisted upon coming to tell the people of our Empire that the mother country is as much attached to them as they are to her, and it is to all the French of North Africa that I bring the salute of France.

It is from Tunis that this friendly message must come, first because Tunis, like Algeria and Morocco, constitutes the firm basis of this Empire where waves the tricolor, where lives the spirit of liberty and justice, but above all, because Tunis is the great frontier country of our North African bloc. It is not our habit to look further than the limits that have been fixed by history. From this town of Tunis we can see the old land of North Africa, from Agadir to Gabès, with its eighteen millions of men—in its geographical, political and human variety, in its material and moral unity, in its infinite resources.

A few moments ago, having the honor to be received by His Highness the Bey, receiving in my turn the delegations of all classes of the population, listening to the moving declarations of the French and Tunisian Presidents of the Grand Council, and lastly, hearing the wise words of France's representative accredited to the Regency, I found the highest and most moving confirmation of this unity and loyalty.

All those who have accompanied me cannot fail to recognize as I did the value and far-reaching consequences of this enthusiasm, this unshakable allegiance that I perceive with joy and the expression of which I hear and accept with pride. This mutual attachment, this free expression of the will of men, are they not marvelous consecrations? The impression of their grandeur will remain deeply engraved in our minds and our hearts.

The variety of the territories of North Africa is the striking proof of the spirit of justice that actuates France. But their unity is realized naturally by virtue of their own genius and the power of the spirit that comes to them from the mother country. This spirit is that of human fraternity and liberty. In the course of centuries it has unified the French community around the same ideal; today it unifies our Empire, it performs again the same miracle of civilization and humanity on a still larger scale.

It is this spirit that points to the future of all our North Africa. It conveys to us, this spirit of France, that each land bears in itself its own genius, but that, to expand, this genius needs the synthesis of all human varieties. It gives to all those who live on the same soil a sentiment of brotherhood that surpasses all other brotherhoods. It does not only bring to the bonds which link men together the justification of the past, but the justification of the future. We want to be, we shall be, the men of this future.

Look around you in the immense world: All the great civilizations that extend beyond the oceans have derived their force from this spirit of fraternity and collaboration. That is what renews empires and makes new cities rise from the ground. It believes in the collaboration of men and permits them to create, by their joint endeavor, a new order conceived in freedom.

What a great task is yours! Time has cemented in an indestructible way the union of France and her Empire. It is the duty of the French government to see that, between all the lands of the Empire, contacts become more frequent and that mutual understandings link and weave them together—as happened in the course of our history between the different French provinces themselves.

In our time the power of nations, their radiance and their prestige, demands that their faculties of production, their initiative, their creative energies be ordered in a sensible and harmonious collaboration. I am then, in my turn, entitled to say to you: with vision give thought to your abilities and your need of one another; do not allow, through lack of foresight, competition that only engenders fatal oppositions; raise your potentialities of production to their maximum in every sphere; develop boldly, usefully, rapidly, all the riches that you possess.

It is to this great work that France wants to contribute all her might and the vigilance of her friendship. She brings you order and discipline, which are the surest and most efficacious protection against brutal force. She brings you her own experience of fraternity and liberty.

She has the strength to insure your security. Her power is invincible though she is a lover of peace. How could I omit to remark here that the strength of our metropolitan army is increased by that of our African army—an association that provides an invaluable school of friendship and devotion between French and Moslems?

[164]

Tunis

France will never permit your effort to be diverted from its goal, which is to create here, in this African land, a human community similar to the French community, inspired by this universal ideal which alone can save men from servitude because it rests on the collaboration of all spiritual values.

Mr Resident General, I would ask you to express my thanks to His Highness the Bey for his welcome, and to tell him that in the name of the President of the Republic, in my own name, and in that of the French government that we wish him good health and a long and prosperous reign.

And I would ask you, gentlemen, to give the people you represent the assurance of the most cordial and the most faithful sentiments of France.

Speech delivered January 4, 1939, at the great banquet given by the Resident General, at the Hotel Majestic in Tunis.

TUNIS

III

IT IS 20h.25,[1] Tunisian time, and since daybreak I have gone from village to village, or more exactly from block-house to blockhouse, along the fortified line built by our military engineers to defend our Tunisian frontiers. What extraordinary spectacles have passed before my eyes!

I shall specially remember, around noontime, a parade remarkable as much for the enthusiasm of the soldiers as for that of the crowd, even more perhaps the touching addresses from the chiefs of the southern tribes who had come with their men voluntarily to witness this parade and take part in it with all their heart and who said to me, when leaving and shaking hands with me: "If one day France needs us again, we will come with all our strength, our soul, our love for her."

Then, I insisted upon visiting new towns that have been, in a short time, built towards the South, towards Libya, and I was surprised to see at Mareth and Ben Gar-dan, at thirty kilometers from the Libyan frontier, popu-

[1] 8:25 P.M.

lations just as enthusiastic as the ones I had met in northern Tunis.

Everywhere I was welcomed by Tunisian children who on my arrival sang the Marseillaise; everywhere the populations were crowding on the route of France's representative, and everywhere our army gave that impression of force and energy that is not surpassed, I think, by any army in the world.

Tomorrow I shall go on my voyage towards Sousse, Sfax, then Bizerte. But tonight, I want to say that it really is in North Africa that one comes to understand the true grandeur of France. She has made order and discipline respected; but she has also made her genius for liberty loved, and I should like to finish by saying that in this noble work all Frenchmen have participated.

I should like to convey my gratitude, not only to the planters, medical men, civil servants of all ranks, but also to those Tunisians who understood us from the first days and collaborated with us in brotherly friendliness.

I should like, moreover, to pay to our glorious African army—this magnificent army already so rich in noble traditions—the homage it deserves. It has given France eminent chiefs, remarkable soldiers, but it has had, above all, the great merit to understand that it was not enough to

[167]

be strongly installed in a great country, but it was necessary to serve, to help and love it, for love only answers love.

It is the grandeur of the French African army to have devoted itself to this noble ideal, and I desire to address to chiefs and men, from this town of Gabès from which I am speaking, the gratitude of the government of the Republic.

Extemporary address, January 4, 1939, from the balcony of Gabès Town Hall.

ALGERIA

Having expressed *his gratefulness to the Algerian population for their welcome, to their politicians for their addresses, having congratulated Governor General Le Beau for his administration and the officers of the African army for the splendid appearance of their troops, and having told of his admiration for them, M. Daladier went on to say:*

How right you were! Indeed, I think only of France. As for myself, I am indifferent about my political destiny. Whether or not I am Prime Minister, what does it matter! But what does matter to me is, to be worthy of the Frenchmen who came before me, worthy of the sons who will come after us; what matters to me is, not to endanger the inheritance left to me, so that, in my turn, I can give the material and moral legacy to those who will come in the future! This resolution, all Frenchmen understand.

I am not blaming the violent polemics to which some speakers have alluded. I should almost be tempted to rejoice and thank the attackers. Once more, thanks to violent men beyond our frontiers, France has been revealed to the French. I have seen evidence of this during my voyage in Tunis, which has been all too short for me. What has perhaps struck me most, is not the welcome of Tunis, so enthusiastic, so unanimous, it is not the acclamations of all these men gathered to see France's representative; but it is to have seen in the territories of the South, across the desert, in the most remote and poorest parts, the children of all tribes who upon my appearance started to sing the Marseillaise, the national hymn of the French and Republicans.

I respect all peoples. I extend the hand of France to all nations. But I feel entitled to ask if there are many other men in the world who can say what I am saying today of France and love. France's policy is to enlighten the peoples who put their confidence in her. Never have we committed acts that will one day come up for judgment in history. We have acted as a generous and free people. It is to the glory of the men who have built this French Empire that we are able to say that, through all vicissitudes, they never thought of anything but to establish it on the closest and most human collaboration between all other peoples and the French people, who were endeavoring to show the way along the same difficult road to progress by which they had themselves once traveled.

Let everyone come to the tribunal of humanity. We shall come with the testimony you bore this morning at this parade of our troops. With this testimony of the great Arab and Kabyl chiefs who are now listening to me, we shall be able to hear calmly the judgment passed upon us by all the peoples of the world.

The union of the French is an accomplished fact! The union of France and her Empire is the great event we are celebrating today. I thought it truly admirable, the day before yesterday, while we were reviewing the troops of the Tunisian South, when the great caïds of the South with their men, who are not soldiers but had come forward voluntarily, came to tell me: "If France is in need of us, let her call: we shall come with all our sons."

I am not seeking flattery for France. I am not asking for homage to the man who represents her today. I am asking all those who followed this voyage to present the simple truth, without hiding or adding anything. In conclusion, I should like to tell you that my wish is that as many Frenchmen as possible should come to Algeria, to Tunis—now a sort of frontier region—and to Morocco and measure there the grandeur of their country.

In Defense Of France

I should also like to tell you that I will oppose, during the days and hours to come, the same attitude not only toward ambitious schemes, but also toward more or less underhand methods, to which apparently some would have recourse. When I said that I would maintain the integrity of this Empire, I meant that I would not be duped, that I would not yield one acre of the lands of this Empire. I meant that I would not let myself be made a fool of by the legal pretexts that some would plead. There is no right against the right of France.

Thus, you see, it is unnecessary for me to say more. We have but one desire—that of living in peace with all countries. To maintain peace, we have made heavy sacrifices; we consented to them. We wished to make them. We have simply followed the dictates of reason. That fact will be realized in the weeks to come; but if we consented to these sacrifices, let it be known—and these will be my last words—that any attempt against this Empire, whether direct or indirect, whether by force or cunning, will be opposed by a determination and will that nothing can conquer.

Speech delivered January 7, 1939, at the Summer Palace in Algiers.

THE DEFENSE OF FRANCE

MUNICH

GENTLEMEN, in the course of the weeks we have just lived through, the world has been anxiously wondering whether it would be plunged into war. Today, coming to give you an account of what has been done, I can say that in this crisis we have saved Peace.

Lately I have said little, because there was only time for action. I was even reproached with being the most silent man in France. In this moment of respite which marks the start of a new plan of action, I want to explain the events that took place and how we faced them.

When this government was formed, the Sudeten problem already existed. The realization of the Anschluss had made the situation more tense.

Already the Czechoslovakian government had announced the publication of a statute of nationalities and Herr Henlein set forth the demands of the Sudeten Germans in eight clauses.

The drama had begun. From the very first days we tried to prevent events that might drag us towards an irremediable conclusion. At that time, on several occasions I publicly defined the position of my government and said: "We are now divided between two equally strong sentiments: the desire of not being compelled to resort to armed intervention, and the will not to break our word if, unfortunately, our hope was disappointed."

In London, as early as the end of April, M. Georges Bonnet and myself revealed our anxieties to the British government and also how we should conceive a settlement in Central Europe. We had the satisfaction of seeing that the British government was not indifferent to these problems. Together we fixed the basis of a collaboration. In our mind there was no question of waiting for the accomplished fact to take action, so that we might have either to redress it with bloodshed or bear it with shame. It was a question of foreseeing events and trying to prevent them.

That is why we acted together immediately, at the time of the crisis of the 21st of May. I insist on reminding you that it was then settled with the good will for peace of all the powers concerned.

From the end of May to September there was a sort of international truce. But in Sudetenland the rise of passions was paving the way for other events.

Then, in a spirit of friendship, we advised the Czechoslovakian government to grant the Sudeten Germans important, just and quick concessions within the framework of their constitution.

The action of the British government was taken simultaneously with ours. The mission of Lord Runciman in Prague gave rise to hope, by affording the opportunity for direct contacts between Czech statesmen and Sudeten chiefs.

Alas, it is nevertheless necessary to record that there was never any synchronization between the propositions of the Czech government, which became more and more extensive, and the demands of the Sudeten Germans, which became more and more importunate.

At the beginning of September, after the speech of the Nuremberg Congress and the announcement by Herr Henlein of the rupture of the negotiations between the Sudeten German delegates and the Prague government, the situation seemed for the first time irremediably compromised.

The German demands were put forward in violent terms. They took, as a basis, the self-determination of all peoples. They appealed to public opinion by the descriptions in the German press of the alleged terror in Sudetenland.

In Defense Of France

Were the forces of war going to get the advantage over the forces of peace? At no time did I think of giving way, of abandoning the country to blind forces that would have led to catastrophe, instead of stemming the tide by the will of men.

That is why, in the night of September 13–14, I entered into conversation with Mr Neville Chamberlain. I told him what I thought of the usefulness of direct contacts between responsible men instead of written relations and exchange of notes. The British Prime Minister, to whom the same thought had occurred at the same time, then went to Berchtesgaden.

In his speech in the House of Commons, Mr Chamberlain asked his colleagues with emotion whether they thought his voyage incompatible with the dignity of his function as Prime Minister. Today I desire to associate the French Parliament with the House of Commons, and to say that, by his courageous initiative and all his actions during the days and nights that followed, Mr Neville Chamberlain well served the cause of peace.

What followed the Berchtesgaden meeting, you already know. In an official report all documents will be collected, all proceedings recorded, all negotiations described. But this book will contain very little hitherto unpublished matter, for it is perhaps the first time in the history of international relations that everything was done publicly and discussed with the full knowledge of the peoples. And I think I can say that if finally peace was saved, we owe it to the abandonment of secret diplomacy. We acted in full daylight, under the influence of public opinion, and I affirm here that the peoples, all peoples, want peace.

Gentlemen, in his conversation with Herr Hitler, Mr Chamberlain had been able to measure the importance of the German demands. As early as Sunday, September 18, in London, he gave me his impressions and his convictions.

We met and deliberated. We studied maps.

The British government let us know the opinion of Lord Runciman. Need I tell you, gentlemen, with what emotion we learned that in his soul and in his conscience the English observer came to the conclusion that it was impossible for the Czechs and the Sudeten Germans to live together in the same territory, when all our efforts had tended toward a federation of Czechoslovakia that would secure the integrity of her territory?

But we had to face realities. We were then placed in the following dilemma:

Either say "No" to the Sudeten demands and, therefore, encourage the Czech government to intransigence and the German government to aggression, provoke an armed conflict that would have as an immediate consequence the destruction of Czechoslovakia herself; or else try to find a compromise through negotiation.

Had we taken the first course of action, who would dare assert that the integrity of Czechoslovakia would have been maintained after a terrible war, even after a terrible war in which there was coalition, even a victorious one?

We chose peace. The London plan was the outcome of this choice.

But, at the same time that we were submitting to Czechoslovakia some painful propositions, we were bringing her the pledge of Great Britain and France to associate ourselves in an international guarantee, because we had obtained from the British government a pledge of the help of its power and prestige in the maintenance of peace and order in the very heart of Europe.

When we left London, we certainly had the feeling that our plan would give rise to indignant protests from Prague, but would perhaps obtain the assent of Berlin.

The Czech government, in its heroic devotion to the cause of peace, accepted the plan.

Munich

But at Godesberg, Herr Hitler in his interview with Mr Chamberlain put forward, with different modalities, new demands. That is how the negotiation which began in an endeavor to find a compromise and with the decision of Mr Chamberlain and mine to establish direct contacts with the German government was brought to a standstill in the night of September 23–24. During the days that followed, Europe was on the brink of catastrophe.

What was the situation at the moment when Mr Chamberlain, after a tempestuous meeting at Godesberg, went back to London?

We had offered Germany the cession of territories whose population was more than 50 per cent German, in accordance with modalities and a regular plan fixed by an international commission. We had provided for the organization of an exchange of the populations, and we were bringing Czechoslovakia a new international guarantee.

What, then, did Germany demand? The immediate cession of the territories, the creation of vast zones of plebiscite, without giving real guarantees to the populations themselves, without giving any international guarantee to the new Czechoslovakia. One might have thought that for Germany it amounted to an operation with all the characteristics and consequences of a conquest, save the recourse to arms.

The difference between the London plan and the Godesberg memorandum was then obvious. The Godesberg memorandum was different both fundamentally and in its form. Was that going to lead to a European war?

During these anxious days, gentlemen—as we all witnessed—there were two currents of opinion in our country. We could feel both of them in every political party, in every trend of public opinion, we can even say that, according to the trend of events, they were contending for the mind and heart of every Frenchman. Some people pinned their faith to negotiation, others to intransigent firmness.

Personally, as head of the government, I recognized at once in these two currents of opinion the infallible instinct of the French people, and I felt that the truth lay in the blending of these two currents and not in their contradiction.

What the people of France wanted was to avoid the irreparable. The irreparable was German aggression. This aggression might have meant the outflow of France's help and assistance; and we should then have asked you to face France's engagements.

Munich

So as not to be surprised by a coup, before the development of German preparations we decided, September 24, on a certain number of military measures whose reason was, not a sort of provocation, but the necessity to put the country in a state of defense, to face whatever events might come. We did everything to insure the adequate defense of the country. Our military chiefs made sure that our forces would be equipped to fulfill their supreme duty to the country.

In London, where we conferred with the British government, General Gamelin gave technical details concerning the effort we had made and the one we might be called upon to accomplish. English and French, we were, all of us, determined in our common will for a peaceful settlement and in our common will to resist aggression.

On the evening of September 26, whatever may have been said, in an official bulletin to the press London declared that if Germany attacked Czechoslovakia, France would go to her assistance and that "Great Britain and Russia would certainly stand by France."

While, in the United States, President Roosevelt raised his voice in a generous and reasonable appeal urging a peaceful settlement, Mr Neville Chamberlain, in full agreement with us, was addressing a new communication to Chancellor Hitler.

In Defense Of France

On September 27, Sir Horace Wilson came back to London, bringing the answer from the Reichsführer. It left little room or time for negotiation. In the House of Commons Mr Neville Chamberlain himself declared that the Chancellor had informed the British messenger that he was determined to act on the following day, September 28, at 2 P.M.

One may laugh and joke. We neither laughed nor joked. We had only a few hours left for action. The broadcast speech of Mr Chamberlain warned the world of the critical aspect of the situation. We resolved to make a last attempt. In the night of September 27–28, we instructed our ambassador in Berlin to ask for a personal audience with Chancellor Hitler. We also requested our ambassador in London to ask Lord Halifax if instructions might be given to the British ambassador in Rome to approach Signor Mussolini and obtain his support for the holding of a conference. We were thus entering into the spirit of the second message of President Roosevelt who so generously helped to make possible a peaceful solution.

At 11:15 A.M., September 28, M. François Poncet was received by Chancellor Hitler and brought him, in the name of the French government, precise proposals with a view to immediate and practical application. Herr Hitler did not set aside our suggestions. He intended to send a written reply.

On his side Mr Chamberlain proposed a last effort for a conference in Germany of the heads of the four governments of the great western powers. Signor Mussolini supported this demand strongly and successfully. He obtained a decisive result: the postponement for twenty-four hours of the German mobilization.

Herr Hitler immediately sent the invitations to the Munich conference.

I accepted this invitation. It was not a question of procedure or of possible counterproposals. It was a question of safeguarding peace that many already thought definitely lost. I said "Yes" and do not regret it.

Indeed, I would have preferred that all the powers concerned be present. But we had to act very rapidly—the least delay might have proved fatal. Was not a frank conversation with Herr Hitler and Signor Mussolini better than written proposals and discussions?

You know the results of the Munich conference, which had more the character of a useful conversation than of a formal conference.

In Defense Of France

We have avoided the resort to force. We have—and there can be no doubt as to this—provoked in four countries the plebiscite of peace. From the spontaneous and warm welcome given in Berlin, Rome, London and Paris by the peoples of the four capitals to the heads of the four governments, and the preponderance of evidence that reached them from many cities and villages of their countries, how could anyone doubt, for one moment, the immense relief of humanity and its attachment to peace?

Essential victory of peace, moral victory of peace—that is the first point I want to bring out. Human victory too, since the Munich agreement, thanks to reciprocal concessions and the good will of all, shows definite progress over the Godesberg memorandum. It mentions the right of option for individuals; it eliminates all stipulations that might have appeared in an armistice imposed by the victor on the vanquished.

We brought to the Czech nation the support of international guarantees. France and Great Britain pledged themselves immediately and without reservations. Germany and Italy, on the other hand, pledged themselves to give guarantees as soon as the question of the Polish and Hungarian minorities in Czechoslovakia had been settled. I am convinced that, thanks to direct conversations, an honorable and fair settlement will soon be found.

An international commission has been created with a view to avoiding unilateral arbitrary decisions.

We can thus hope to substitute the practices of right for the solutions of force. If tomorrow some English and French contingents are called upon to go to the contested districts, they will do so with the feeling that they spare these regions and the world the ordeal of war.

Certainly the Munich agreement reduces Czechoslovakia's territory. But Czechoslovakia can pursue her own free life and we will do our best to help her. Few states, in the course of history, have accepted such painful sacrifices for the cause of peace.

Czechs and Slovaks are brave peoples. We know that they would have fought to defend the integrity of their country and, their cause failing, would have died with honor in a desperate resistance. But their leading statesmen, President Beneš, M. Hodza and General Sirovy, took the highest view of their duty towards their country and above all towards humanity.

When General Sirovy brought to the Czech people the knowledge of his acceptance of the Munich agreement, he told them that his duty had been to "save the nation's life" in order to allow recovery.

In Defense Of France

We all feel a profound admiration for the moving dignity and wonderful courage of this noble people who have borne and are still bearing such a painful ordeal.

And now, gentlemen, why did we succeed in preventing war at the very time when it seemed ready to break out? Why, as I have just explained, were we able to score a certain number of real advantages and guarantees as opposed to real sacrifices to which we had to consent? Because, in these difficult negotiations, we have always shown our desire for justice and our loyalty. Because we negotiated like men for whom negotiation was not only an unavoidable act of this great international drama, but the real way to peace.

I must at once add, with the same certainty, that if our negotiation succeeded, we owe it, above all, to the fact that we showed our strength. Let there be no misunderstanding: I do not mean that our strength has been a means of intimidation or pressure. You can no more think of intimidating Germany than you can think of intimidating France. But to show your strength is to place yourself in a position to discuss on an equal footing. You can only discuss with a man or a nation if you have first won the respect of your opponent. I felt, from the very moment of my arrival at Munich, the respect of Germany for France. It was based on the knowledge that France was ready to fight to prevent whatever might have been against her vital interest or the interest of justice. What made success possible, therefore, was the resolution France showed.

We must here pay a rightful homage to our dear and great country. At the first call, with an admirable response in which gravity had taken the place of the enthusiasms of old, young troops and veterans of the Great War rejoined their posts and in a few hours had formed the impassable barrier that always has protected the country.

On our frontiers involved in the advance of the troops were those who would have suffered most from the very outbreak of the war. They accepted without a murmur all orders for discipline and security given by the military chiefs. Let us thank them here in the name of France.

During these days our country commanded the esteem of all neighboring peoples: the esteem that rests on the memory of struggles that divided or joined us; the esteem that no war veteran can refuse another, whatever might have been his uniform during the war; the esteem that a great nation, both virile and pacific, always commands.

In Defense Of France

We have now a duty: it is to show that same feeling for the great people who are our neighbors, who were once our enemy, with whom we wish to establish a lasting peace.

No doubt, gentlemen, our outlook on life is widely different from that now accepted in Germany and Italy. But other countries whose ideals are just as different from ours maintain friendly relations with us.

Whatever form of political regime they have chosen, all peoples have the same love for peace; what is important at the present time is to unite the good will for peace which exists all over the world.

I have just recalled the feelings that the French people entertain for the German people, feelings that, in this very House, many of our predecessors had also expressed. This does not signify that we are thinking of renouncing existing collaborations. It is not for us a question of substituting new friendships for old ones.

In the interest of peace we want to add new friendships to old ones and also to renew acquaintance with some nations. I know that for this undertaking we may count upon the friendship between France and Great Britain, which recent events, whatever some may have said, have rendered still more loyal and complete.

Munich

Shall I confess, gentlemen, that the other day, when I arrived at Le Bourget and witnessed the spontaneous joy of the Parisians, which answered the joy of the people of Berlin, Rome and London—shall I confess that I could not help a vague feeling of anxiety? I was thinking that peace is not a permanent conquest, it has to be defended every day.

I certainly appreciate demonstrations of popular rejoicing, although I am not overelated by them; but, as head of the government, I think only of the future of our country.

The safeguarding of peace ought not to encourage relaxation. It must mark, on the contrary, a resurgence of all French energies. I am telling you this with all the strength of my conviction: if the country were to relax, if the maintenance of peace were for it only an excuse for apathy, we should—in less time than you may believe—drift toward dangerous tomorrows. For myself, I could not agree—I am telling you this in all cordiality and frankness—to lead France towards such days.

The most precious possession—the one, in fact, that gives rise to all hopes—has been safeguarded for us. We have maintained peace; let us know how to keep it, let us know how to establish it on unshakable foundations.

In Defense Of France

It is possible, as has been written, that at Munich the face of the world was changed in a few hours. However that may be, there is one certainty: it is that France must face a new situation with a new realization of her duty.

The greatest crime towards the country would be to let political controversies take precedence over resolutions. More than anyone else, perhaps, I would have the right to say what hampered my efforts during these last weeks, what imperiled the efficaciousness of my course of action; but it is my imperative duty to set an example.

At the beginning of this declaration I spoke of the two great currents of opinion which passed through our country during this crisis as converging manifestations of the same will. I would not—I could not—distinguish the one from the other. They have become part of the stirring emotion that sent to the colors all the sons of the country, whatever their social conditions, their religious beliefs, their personal convictions.

The French, who all want to save France, must now consider themselves in a permanent state of mobilization for the cause of peace and for the country. The first duty of everyone is to work with all his might at the task that claims him.

We shall maintain peace only if our production allows

us to speak on an equal footing with the peoples around us.

We shall maintain peace only if we have healthy finances and if we can count upon the whole resources of the nation.

We shall maintain peace only if we at last draw up the plan of a general settlement, if we organize Europe and the world on new principles, and if, after having avoided war in Central Europe, we compel it to fall back wherever it is still raging.

We shall maintain peace only if we strengthen the union of hearts and minds which common anxieties have brought close together. Anything that incites hatred, anything that sets the French against one another, can now be considered only as treason.

This country must undergo a moral transformation. For a few days, grouped round its mobilized forces, it has found its unity again. My dear friends, let us not waste this spirit of union in sterile disputes and secondary polemics.

In order to carry this task of recovery to a successful issue, the government must be in a position to act. We have decided to ask you for the means of action.

It rests with you to grant or to refuse them. But I am

asserting again that the interest, the very life of the country is at stake.

Speech delivered in the Chamber of Deputies, October 4, 1938.

AFTER THE COUP

I THINK THE HIGH ASSEMBLY will agree with the government that the present circumstances call less for speeches than for action.

We are, in fact—we must tell the truth to the country—confronted by a very grave situation, which might rapidly become a dramatic situation. Our duty is to face it with resolution, energy and courage.

A moment ago I heard a speaker criticize the attitude of the government last September as well as the agreement it concluded at Munich. Gentlemen, I regret that I have no intention of presenting any apologies, either in the Senate or in the Chamber of Deputies.

I will remark for those who criticize, who are sometimes carried away by an eagerness that is no doubt generous, that France is the only country who then mobilized more than a million men, who would have been followed by other millions had there been a coup. But when, after the inquiry set up in Czechoslovakia, men of a friendly neighboring state had testified to their na-

[195]

tion and other countries that life in the same land seemed impossible for Germans and Czechs, we thought it better to negotiate and to try to insure both the maintenance of peace in Europe and a compromise making life possible for Czechs and Slovaks. That is what we wanted to do, and it is an effort that I do not regret having attempted.

Neither do I regret the declaration of Franco-German collaboration signed last winter by the German government and the representative of the French government. What politician, what French veteran has not dreamed of a policy of collaboration with the foe of yesterday? What head of a responsible government in France has not endeavored at least to ease the relations between these two great peoples?

I tried this, as many of my predecessors had done, and I am not at all ashamed to have for months given all my strength in an attempt to ward off the threat of war.

This example, given to the country and to the world, today authorizes us to say that we are now in the trench which we must defend at the cost of whatever sacrifice.

The Munich agreement? Destroyed. The mutual declaration of Franco-German collaboration? Violated in letter and spirit. All this has disappeared, and with it

—in violation of engagements undertaken—has disappeared from the map of Europe a friendly country of
which I shall not speak at length, as words would only
be vain. But I think members of the Senate will understand and share our emotion before the spectacle of
these tragic events.

Today, and in the hours to come, we shall have to
face events that may develop dangerously. That is why
the government is asking frankly for full special powers,
and I declare to the High Assembly, as I have done in
the Chamber, that it would be impossible for me to accept any emasculation of the bill by elimination of any
portion of the text or by any amendment to it.

As M. Caillaux has said, it is not a question of full
powers, which many governments have often asked from
the two Assemblies. The object is not to act by decrees
to modify taxes; it is not a question of facing any special
financial situation. The motives for this demand for full
powers are different. It is a question of facing a grave
situation that may, as I have said, become dramatic.

I regret that I am not in agreement with some of the
speakers who preceded me. I do not think it possible
normally to compete with states which have at least the
advantage of being able to move quickly and with abso-

lute secrecy. How can we save democracy? How can we save the Republic? Do you think that in these tormented times we have just lived in, in these tragic hours which we have just gone through we can work with the old methods that were good in the old days, or would still be in normal times? This is the storm, gentlemen, and we must face it with all the means the situation requires and with our will and the will of the French people.

These measures are all of a nature to insure the defense of the country.

First, military measures. I think that, in a few minutes, the Advisory Committee will meet, study and ratify, if needs be, measures that I shall propose tomorrow at the meeting of the Cabinet.

Economic measures too. Why try to evade it? I realize how many senators, how many deputies, feel a sort of discomfort when we ask for a great supplementary effort of work; but here it is the country's safety that has to be considered before the comfort of the citizens.

It is correct, as M. Bachelet, I think, was recalling, that some of our decrees have provided the means for a considerable increase in production in some arsenals or factories working for national defense.

After The Coup

Gentlemen, I would here pay homage to the working class, which has answered our appeal, and which, in some industries, works more than forty-eight hours and sometimes more than fifty hours for national defense.

If I ask you now for special powers, it is because I have not the means, with existing legislation, of imposing the same system, if it becomes necessary, on all private industries which, in a direct or indirect way, will have to devote their forces to national defense.

Economic measures? Financial measures too, which we must apply without any delay, for all these decisions will of course occasion heavy expenditure.

Can you conceive, gentlemen, the necessity for me to go before each committee, each House, for hours, for days, while at our door events make the urgency more and more pressing? In conscience, this is impossible! No head of government in my place, I am convinced, could do without the vote of special powers.

You may reply then: Why this government? Why did you not enlarge your cabinet? Why did you not recruit new ministers from every party?

There are two reasons. The first is that I have no time to waste in discussions and sterile arguments.

If this reason does not seem sufficient, there is another

one. Yesterday it was certain qualified speakers in the Chamber of Deputies, and not I, who declared that they did not want this increase in the ranks of the cabinet and that they preferred to entrust the special powers to the present government, reserving for themselves the right to pass judgment on its actions—for parliamentary discussion should never be paralyzed. To my mind, this is a more efficacious program than the one consisting of trying to find a solution in political mixtures, balances or disproportions, in gathering round a table where it is much less a question of debating the pros and cons of this or that measure than one of coming to a decision on the strongest and quickest measures!

That is why, gentlemen, the government is asking you to grant these powers, it is asking you to give the means of facing promptly those events to which you have referred. I do not think that the Capitol is imperiled; I do not think that the Republic is in danger—I mean from within. But it *would* be in danger if France had to bear severe defeats, because its destiny is linked with that of France!

Allow me to tell you that I have nothing to deny or regret in my political life, I have loyally served all prime ministers who called on me to enter their cabinet.

After The Coup

But I might recall, if I wanted to let myself be dragged into vain polemics, that when I asked for the same loyal co-operation I received nothing but party replies and almost excommunication.

But let us put these aside. They are only vain polemics, sterile quarrels.

Let us now show Europe that we have our backs to the wall and can only get out of this intricate situation by going straight ahead. That is all I have to tell the Senate.

I have already this morning received communications from France's representatives in foreign countries, informing me that the vote of special powers by the Chamber, in the circumstances that accompanied it, has made the most favorable impression on our friends abroad.

We must strengthen this impression. We must work up all our diplomatic agreements with frankness and precision.

We must adjust all our forces. That is the task of the government.

I need not tell you today, gentlemen, that I have but one single preoccupation—for the Republic and the country; that questions of power or government leave me indifferent when I measure the responsibility placed upon me which pledges, more than my life, the honor of my name and my people.

That is why I am asking you for an overwhelming vote.

That is why I am asking you for a vote so conclusive that this spirit of comfort which begins to revive again, this renaissance of hope which begins to manifest itself in Europe, will be confirmed by the decision of the French senate.

There is a heavy task in front of us. We have to insure the country's safety, the safety of republican freedom, otherwise than by words: we have to insure it by action. We must have that which gives value to the life of men, whatever their country, the great ideal of justice and liberty.

Speech delivered in the Senate, March 19, 1939.

FRANCE AND HER WILL

As head of the government responsible for French policy, it is first as a man that I want to speak to the French and, beyond the frontiers of my country, to all in the world who possess a loyal and generous heart. There is a language that needs no translation to be understood by all: it is the language of the heart. If we were face to face—you, who are now listening to me with your children near you, I, speaking to you with the thought of my sons near me—we would understand one another at the very moment when our glances would meet. We would know that we feel in the same way the present difficulties and threatening dangers, as also the same hope for the future. There would be no need for words for us to understand that we think, all of us, only of the maintenance of peace with honor and independence for our country.

Each of us is wondering whether his country is not threatened, whether our neighbors are safe. This uncertainty compels governments to take precautionary measures. Treaties are signed, but before they even

[203]

come into force they cease to be a guarantee for one party, an obstacle for the other. Those who do not act feel in some way the accomplices of force, and those who act have the fear of provoking it. Everywhere the frenzy of armaments destroys all other activities. How could men still act and think freely?

Anxiety giving rise to anxiety, armaments calling for more armaments—it was by a similar fatality that, many times, war broke out.

This situation dictates my duty to me. I have to tell you this evening what France wants, what is her strength and her resolution.

What does France want? Peace for free men.

France's moral strength? It is her material and moral unity, once more realized in the face of peril.

France's resolution? It is to defend her ideal and rights.

To make everyone understand such primary truths, a prime minister does not spend time in vain polemics.

It will be nothing new for the French now listening to me, but it may be news for foreigners if I say that the union of France has never been so deep, so complete as today.

It is not true, of course, what some men repeat, whose mission is to spread throughout the world the absurd

France And Her Will

fable of France's impotence or her abdication. Never has she been more united, more resolute, never has she been stronger.

She hopes that peace will be saved, for she hates war. But, if war were imposed on her, if it were for her the only alternative between downfall and dishonor, she would rise and spring to arms for the defense of her liberty.

This liberty she is in a position to defend.

Alarmed by the European and world disorder, the French have understood that, to save their country, a great effort was necessary. They have accomplished it.

Increased production, healthy and severe economy of our public finances, acceptance of indispensable sacrifices have already given good results. Our economic situation is improving, as the figures of French production show.

The franc has remained firm on the basis we have fixed. National defense is strongly guaranteed.

The present international crisis has, therefore, not taken by surprise a France weak and bewildered. On the contrary, in spite of this crisis, France pursues her task on the way to recovery. Her production is increasing and unemployment decreasing. Her currency is one of the strongest. Yesterday, again, the franc rose on all exchanges, and we received, for only that one day, more than four tons of gold. For we had felt deeply that to a growing danger France had to oppose an increased strength.

It was because I had clearly the vision of this necessity that I asked Parliament for special powers for the period during which peace might be imperiled.

Why did I ask for special powers?

Why did Parliament grant them to me?

Because we had to act and not to discuss. Because it was imperative to take rapidly and silently the exceptional measures necessary for the defense of the country.

By our recent decrees, completing the ones that came into force last autumn, we have decided to increase still more the work of the country, to subordinate all private interests to the idea of public safety, the only interest which must at present dominate French consciences.

We have also taken military measures to which the nation answered with a virile resolution, as it had done at all dangerous periods of its history.

No one refuses to make the effort which we are asking, because all know that France is a just nation who will not found the necessities of her defense on the misery of her sons.

France And Her Will

Had we remained passive, had the country remained apathetic, had the government not assumed its responsibilities, all affirmations of our rights would soon only be vain rhetoric, while our force was stronger than ever.

The strength of France? Do you know what it is?

It is the whole of the magnificent army whose chiefs and men, taught by a long experience, united by the same thought, form a unified bloc without losing any of their individual virtues.

The strength of France? It is in a rich countryside that it finds its support, in a balanced climate and production, a soil fertilized by the tenacious effort of agricultural people and which shelters her from possible distress and famine.

The strength of France? It is present in the whole world, in our most remote possessions where, as Minister for the Colonies, fifteen years ago, I had already felt the most ardent loyalty. It is proportionate to that immense Empire, whose African bloc is the main pivot of resistance and whose affectionate attachment and total devotion to the mother country I have recently been able to measure.

The strength of France? It is not only made of this material power, but of all spiritual and moral values as great today as at any time of our history; it is this constant striving for human dignity, liberty and order; it is the fraternity of all creeds and all ideals; it is the spontaneous union of a whole people seeking truth and justice, even in its political quarrels, but which has no need of a formal reconciliation to unite in an hour of peril.

The strength of France? It is the friendships of France, those which consecrate our agreements as well as those which spontaneously associate her with free peoples and with suffering peoples.

In the present upheaval of the world some new definitions of life are offered to peoples in anguish to cover the oldest practices and expedients. Servitude is called liberty, submission is called voluntary adhesion, despair is called pride of life. Destruction of human values is termed progress. Humanity is led to its ruin under false appearances of salvation.

May I tell you, in France's name, what service of country and humanity really is? It is never to sacrifice men in vain; never to crush them under the servitudes of pride and force; it is to allow them, under the protection of the nation, to live according to their own will, to believe according to their own heart, to think according to their genius, to act according to their conscience.

It is because we believe in all this that we shall never admit that relations between nations should be ruled by force. What rules these relations for us French is, first, justice and right, and only when these disappear, and a wave of violence breaks loose, does the recourse to force become a primary duty.

Pacific and powerful, France can face the future with confidence.

She hears with serenity fierce demands sometimes reverberating around her, because she knows that negotiation should only throw light on her rights and that violence against her should be overcome.

Why not tackle the problem bravely? The whole world is expecting me tonight to speak of Franco-Italian relations.

I will; and with complete frankness—or, rather, I have only to let facts speak for themselves.

To bring to an end prolonged misunderstandings, on January 7, 1935, Franco-Italian agreements were signed in Rome. They were intended to "settle definitely," to "liquidate" the differences between the two countries.

Some agreements had intervened by which Italy obtained in Africa rectifications of frontiers, cessions of territories and economic facilities; France, a progressive transformation of the statute concerning the Italians in Tunis, gradually, in 1945, 1955, 1965.

France began to put these agreements into force. Never were they questioned again, either during the Abyssinian conquest or after, or in official conversations in the spring of 1938, or at the time of the recognition of the Italian Empire and the nomination of M. François Poncet as our ambassador in Rome.

It was only by a letter dated December 17 last that Count Ciano informed us that he no longer considered as valid these 1935 agreements.

On the other hand, I am going to quote the words of Signor Mussolini in his speech of last Sunday:

"We do not ask the world to judge, but we want the world to be informed.

"In the Italian note of December 17, 1938, Italian problems with regard to France were clearly defined, problems with a colonial character. These problems have a name. They are: Tunis, Djibuti, Suez."

This declaration has caused a great surprise in international circles.

The reference to the letter of December 17 has induced people to believe that this document contained

Italian claims in detail. A press campaign has led people to understand that France had, on that date, been presented with concrete demands to which she had not answered.

We are going to publish the letter of December 17. You will be able to read it *tomorrow* in the papers, followed by the answer which we forwarded to the Italian government a few days later.

But I wanted to bring you, as early as tonight, the declaration that the letter did not contain any such details, nor were Suez, Djibuti and Tunis brought into question.

What, then, does the Italian letter purport? Simply that Italy considers as no longer valid the 1935 treaty, and she endeavors to justify this attitude.

The essential argument invoked is the following: the conquest of Abyssinia and the foundation of the Italian Empire are alleged to have created new rights for Italy.

There is no need to tell you that we cannot accept this argument! What does it really mean? It means that each new conquest or new concession would create new rights. Thus the claims that might be presented to us would practically be boundless, since each of them, once satisfied, would engender future claims.

[211]

In Defense Of France

Moreover, I repeat that none of these claims was put forward in the letter of December 17.

Will it be maintained that these claims were presented to us in the form of press articles and street demonstrations? In that case I shall only have to answer that France's position was immediately made public. I have said, and I maintain, we would yield neither an acre of our lands nor a single one of our rights.

France signed the 1935 agreements. Faithful to her engagements, she is ready to pursue their complete and loyal execution. In the spirit and on the basis of these agreements, which I have here defined and recalled, she does not refuse to examine any propositions that might be made.

Since I am referring to Franco-Italian relations, I also want to deny legends that are being circulated regarding the situation of the 94,000 Italians who live in Tunis with 108,000 Frenchmen and nearly two and a half million Moslems. It is alleged that these Italians are ill-treated or even persecuted. This is a fable. On the contrary, they are treated in every way most liberally, they and their children. Foreigners of all nationalities who live in Tunis have often testified as to this.

I can myself bear witness to this, since I was in North

France And Her Will

Africa at the beginning of January. I also want, since I am speaking of Tunis, to address my cordial greeting to the noble Moslem population who keep, within the boundaries of our Empire, their centuries-old creed and all the virtues of their civilization. I want to thank them for their moving loyalty and devotion to France. Let them be certain that France will continue to protect them faithfully and vigilantly and that at no time will she tolerate any interference with her mission.

If there were any need to demonstrate further what sense of justice, what sentiments of courtesy the French have towards the Italians, why should I not quote the example of the 900,000 Italians who live on our metropolitan soil? Can they complain of French hospitality? Are they not happy to live under the protection of our laws and enjoy our freedom?

Thus France remains in this field, as in all others, faithful to her highest traditions. In the same way, with regard to another great neighboring people with whom we have had so many conflicts, France has shown continually the same good will.

We signed the Munich agreement and a few months later the Franco-German declaration. Again, a few days ago, inspired by the spirit of this declaration, we sent a mission to Berlin to negotiate an economic agreement, indispensable basis of a lasting collaboration.

But, as I have said in the Senate, the conquest of Czechoslovakia and the occupation of Prague by the German army have struck a heavy blow at our patient endeavor.

For years we had been told about the self-determination of all peoples as a justification for some actions.

Later, we were told of natural fervent desires. . . . We are now hearing about living space, which is only the constant accompaniment of the will to conquer.

There is not now, as a matter of fact, a single man who does not know that war would be a catastrophe for all nations; that there is not one country that would not run the risk of destruction.

We do not want this. We want to help Europe to be saved.

In the name of my country I invite to a confident collaboration all powers who think like us, all who are, like us, ready to persevere in the ways of peace, but who would at once form one bloc against aggression.

I know that these words, which have defined the position of France, will find an echo among friendly countries, across Europe and beyond the Channel and the

France And Her Will

Atlantic. If, for example, the Franco-British collaboration is as complete as it is at present, it is due to the fact
that France and Great Britain have the same views on
these problems. They wish to reach the same goal by the
same means.

I may, therefore, cherish the hope that all reasonable
men—and there are some in every country—will listen to
the language of reason.

They will remember that it is free from threats, and
does not try to humiliate anyone. They will find in it the
proof that France puts all her vigorous and intact forces
to the service of peace.

As for France, our country, nothing will lead her
away from the destiny she chose freely and in the clear
knowledge of her rights and her strength. Once more
she will show the world what work can do when it
serves human dignity; what courage can perform when
it is guided solely by justice; where the spirit of sacrifice
can reach when it is accepted to save liberty.

Speech broadcast March 29, 1939.

COLLABORATION FOR PEACE

AFTER THE RECEPTION of the message from the President of the Republic, inspired by a noble patriotism and a high sense of civic duty, at the hour when the representatives of the nation are here gathered together, it is our first duty to place the safety of the Republic in the hands of those young men who on land, on the sea and in the air protect France against every menace.

At the same time we must offer our homage to the entire nation.

During several weeks she has borne, and she has shown herself resolved to bear for so long as necessary, the burden of an ordeal by which some wished to see her moral resistance enfeebled—as though a nation of liberty could show herself more sensitive to that type of nervous tension than the countries of silence, of constraint and of servitude.

While these young Frenchmen consent resolutely to the effort which is required of them, without giving attention to the foreign propaganda which would like to sow doubts among them, the entire nation exhorts us to show ourselves worthy of her and of her magnificent history. France is a vast workshop, in which from this day forward millions of men will labor without halt or respite to insure the national defense. Our duty is to think of our country alone. Our duty is to make and to maintain the virile resolutions necessary to her safety.

Already, several days ago, I was called upon to explain the sentiments of France. Whatever the complexity and diversity of international problems, in reality only one is before Europe: that of domination or collaboration. The true problem is, in fact, that of learning whether the divergences of interests which may separate peoples are to be decided by methods of peaceful collaboration or by those of violence and force.

Is it necessary to call to mind recent events, in which engagements were violated, agreements torn up, nations destroyed or reduced to slavery, in spite of the most solemn promises given at the same time the decision was made secretly to act in the opposite direction? Is it necessary to call to mind economic demands which are used as a pretext for political exactions? Is it necessary to call to mind that at the very hour when peace is most invoked, when the highest altars are raised to her, armies are mobilizing, fleets plowing the seas, airplanes assembling, and that twenty years after the war, millions of men are once more in arms?

But the love of peace is so profound among all the peoples of the world that they are forced to invoke it to cover the enterprises of force. Does peace, then, consist in invading the territory of other states, in always presenting new demands which could bring on conflict, in condemning peoples to misery by imposing upon them new armaments constantly being increased, which render useless the international collaboration offered to them? All nations which are most attached to the method of free collaboration with all other countries ought to be determined, if necessary, to oppose threats with all their vigilance and firmness. This is the thought, this is the will of France.

This thought, this will, has inspired the action of the government. France is ignorant of hatred. She feels a sincere sympathy toward all peoples. She knows by long experience that war will not resolve any of the present problems, that on the contrary it will render their solution more difficult and more ruinous. She thinks that in a world whose natural resources have been doubled by the inventions of science, every nation can easily achieve its share of happiness, prosperity and liberty.

Collaboration For Peace

The peoples know well—and we are proud to say it—
that France does not menace them, that she desires to
collaborate with all and to dominate none. We have no
need to solicit witnesses from among our neighbors to
prove that we are not contemplating aggression. It is a
long time since, following the noble words of the men
of the French Revolution, France declared peace to the
world. Our policy is exclusively devoted to the assembly
of men and of nations for the defense of peace.

These are the ideas which inspired the negotiations in
which we took part and in which we took the initiative
during recent weeks. The solidarity of Great Britain
and France is firmer, more based on mutual confidence
than ever. It remains the basis of French policy, and we
will not let it be enfeebled either by intrigue or by odious
and lying propaganda. At the moment when, by clear-
sighted and voluntary effort, the British people, breaking an age-old tradition, freely impose upon themselves
the discipline of obligatory military service, the French
people renews its fraternal salute to them. It is with lively
admiration that France has become aware of the noble
message that President Roosevelt addressed to the world
in the name of the great Republic of the United States.
In giving the message its complete support from the first

hour, our government has interpreted the profound feeling of every Frenchman.

Certainly, our country has always affirmed its adhesion to the doctrine which seeks to unite by a general accord all powers desirous of guaranteeing their security. But the experience of the twenty years that have gone by since the war has thrown light on the grave difficulties which the conclusion of such a general accord encounters. The more it seeks to unite the nations, the more it loses in precision and strength, each state seeking to include limitations or preferences. This is why we have contracted precise, simple, clear engagements with the nations that wish to associate themselves with us for the common defense of their vital interests and ours. In other regions of Europe, on the contrary, we have given to certain countries, with the support of Great Britain, a spontaneous and unilateral guarantee. Other negotiations are under way, animated by the same attention to existing realities. I repeat that all peaceful countries have been invited to this collaboration.

Thus, since March 20 we have taken the initiative in letting Rumania know that, if she were the object of aggression, we would immediately come to her assistance. In the same way we have assured Greece of our immediate assistance in case that country were threatened with aggression.

Moreover, following the visit of Colonel Beck to London and the reciprocal guarantees contracted between Great Britain and Poland, we have taken, in accord with that noble and courageous nation, the necessary measures for the immediate and direct application of our treaty of alliance. I remind you today of the declaration I made to the press on April 13. It takes on all its force at the moment when Poland is on guard over her vital national interests.

We are discussing with Turkey the conclusion of a guarantee agreement destined to maintain peace in the eastern Mediterranean, where our interests are alike. We also wish to settle with her, in the most amicable spirit, a problem which has long been undecided between us. The recent visit of General Weygand to Turkey has shown us how profound is the esteem which unites our two nations.

Finally we consider as essentially desirable the participation of the U.S.S.R. in this common work of mutual assistance. The Franco-Soviet treaty, concluded in 1935 and still in force, attests that the pursuit and the maintenance of this participation in equality and reciprocity are among the fixed objectives of our diplomatic action. If certain divergences still remain as to the accompanying details of this accord among the English, French and Russian governments, an understanding was reached at the beginning of the conversations on the basic necessity: the necessity of employing common action for the high interests of peace.

Thus, for the first time, there is realized in Europe and the Near East one of the conditions we have always considered indispensable to the maintenance of peace: community of obligations between France and Great Britain.

Is it necessary to add that this diplomatic effort has no other object but that of assuring liberty and independence to all nations? We wish a peace that respects all rights. Violence or the menace of violence will conduct Europe to catastrophe. In co-operation with all states which wish to live in honor we are resolved to line ourselves up against these things.

A vigilant and firm foreign policy demands the effort of the nation. An easy-going interior policy can reduce it to nothing. Peace is kept or achieved by the determined labor of every day, by the tenacious will of a people resolved upon all sacrifices to maintain its liberty.

Collaboration For Peace

All the rest is nothing but a vain declamation. National defense is a bloc. It demands, first, military measures. We have taken them. We are not thinking of reducing them, but rather of reinforcing them, if certain massive mobilizations continue to be maintained beyond our frontiers.

National defense also demands financial, economic and social measures. For the year 1939 alone, we must consecrate more than fifty billions to the salvation of the country. It was, therefore, inevitable that heavy sacrifices should be demanded of French citizens. We have done so with the national safety alone in mind. However rigorous these sacrifices may have been, we can at least declare that the standard of living among our working classes is greatly superior to that which is imposed upon the workers of the great neighboring nations. The franc remains a money in which to take refuge. The returns of gold continue. The Treasury is assured of being able to meet all necessities. The disastrous perspectives of bankruptcy and of inflation have been put aside from our path. Is this not the proof of the effectiveness of the plan whose application we are continuing? We have stimulated French production, brought exports up, improved the collaboration of all the forces of labor.

In Defense Of France

At the moment when I am speaking, the beginning of May, when certain people expected us to be at our weakest, it will suffice to say that there is in France just one business on strike, with a total of thirteen strikers. I desire, from the height of this tribune, to pay homage to the patriotism of the workers of France, to those in the fields and in the cities, to those who have just been recalled to our colors and who are, moreover, assured by our decrees that they will recover their work or their employment when the international situation permits that they be sent back to their homes.

Such is the policy, humane and national, of France. It covers not only the territory of the metropolis but North Africa and the whole of our empire, all of whose sons affirm each day their resolution to defend the great French commonwealth even unto the supreme sacrifice. To this effort we give our true strength, which will permit us to surmount every test, which will permit us to save peace. That strength is in the profound unity of France, the indestructible union of all Frenchmen.

Certain people hope that France, invincible when united, will permit herself to be demoralized by the alternation of threats and promises of peace. It seems as though a new form of war without battles were being used against France, a war of uncertainty, of anxiety renewed and hope deceived. But our will has not yielded and will not yield. We know that what we have to defend are our country and our liberties, our beliefs, our ideal of human dignity. If just and equal peace is desired of us, we are ready to make it. If peace is attacked, the weight of our arms will be felt. If some try to exhaust us by wavering between peace and war, we will hold on as long as necessary. Neither force nor ruse can accomplish anything against France.

Declaration of May 11, 1939.

APPENDIX

A GREAT SERVANT OF THE NATION: VAUBAN

Among all men of the seventeenth century, Vauban is perhaps the one nearest to us. That is not to say that he is a modern man, not of his time. But down the pages of history none has been less obscured, none has remained so easy to understand and so close to the man of today.

Man of the land and of the people of France, man of science, man of substance, he has mainly three preoccupations and impulsions that cannot be alien to us and that still remain the preoccupations and impulsions of our country.

There is something rather appealing and simple about this servant of the Great King. He springs from the lesser nobility of the Morvan, of peasant stock, rural and close to the people. He comes from the land and not from the Court. Saint-Simon said, "At the most, 'Petit gentilhomme de Bourgogne.'"

Up to the age of seventeen he remained in his village, familiar with the peasants, friendly with humble people.

In Defense Of France

He never forgot these ties, these first friendships. Engineer to the king, lieutenant general of the armies, field marshal of France, he found again under him, as trench diggers and land surveyors, these men of the land. He always defended them with energy, he fought for their rights, treated them with humanity and kindness. By virtue of the very character of his work and duties, his connection with these peasant people was never severed, and to his last day he remained among them, more engineer than soldier, commanding men who are at heart laborers and artisans, soldiers to whom the shovel and the pickaxe are the most effective weapons.

Thus, by heart and character, by a simple and direct humanity acquired in the company of humble people, Vauban is near to us. But he is so equally by the quality of his mind. On the battlefields, he created what today we would call the theory of scientific armament. For he is an artilleryman, trench digger, hydrographer, topographer, architect and strategist. His first care was to conduct attacks in such a way as to expose the men as little as possible, to protect them by earthworks and trenches in their very march forward; but his great effort was to reinforce all the frontiers of France, to raise along the natural limits of his country a strong barrier that could stop the invader and insure peace.

He did not want to go beyond these natural limits, between the sea, the Alps, the Pyrenees and the Rhine. Beyond these boundaries he no longer felt safe. In this respect, and taking into consideration the differences of the times, he followed the doctrine of Frenchmen of today, he was preoccupied by the same things as we are today.

Calm in battle, fearless under fire, methodical and considerate, he always retained that same principle in all the great enterprises in which he took part. "I saw him laden with cares at Namur," a great soldier, like him field marshal of France—his friend Catinat—said of him. So when the king, carried away by his victories, looked beyond the reasonable limits of France, Vauban curbed the royal appetite for conquests and insisted that the frontier of France might have the intangible force of reason and logic which is also that of justice.

Few men have left more traces, few have so indelibly marked French soil with their impress. In how many villages, towns, ports along frontiers and coast line can Vauban still be evoked by the remains of a fortress or some great work of engineering? Chance alone does not in this way preserve, at four cardinal points, the memory of a man. This living presence of Vauban, after so many years, after repeated glories, is the mark of his immense accomplishment and the connection between this accomplishment and the country that supported it and to which it gave security. Even more than the work so achieved, of fortresses, ports, canals, town gates, water towers and dikes, it is the mark of a method and a way of thinking, it is one of the modes of expression, of realization and assertion of France and her genius.

Let us, then, follow after three hundred years the life of this man whose labor still keeps its significance.

When seventeen years of age he left his village and served under the banners of Prince of Condé. The victor of Rocroy was then in conflict with the Crown. But Vauban did not stay long among the factionists. He was not a feudal noble, he sprang from titled small landowners, and his instinct directed him to the central power which then represented the state and the nation. At twenty-two he was an engineer to the king and began, on the northern frontier, the long career that was to constitute an essential part of the history of the reign, together with the greatest victories as well as the sudden drives of energy and resistance which limited disasters.

From then on, his task was to seize towns and to defend them. He was a soldier, not an intellectual recluse. It was on this ground, under fire and in the trenches that his science was developed. At the siege of Montmédy only, during attacks that lasted forty days, he was wounded four times and saw, in the very first week, three other engineers to the king fall next to him.

In 1658 he was twenty-five years old. He had already taken command at three sieges: Gravelines, Ypres, Oudenarde. He followed the king in all his campaigns. In 1667 he took Douai and was wounded there. In the same year he took Lille and turned it into a French fortress. At the same time he was given the mission of turning Dunkirk into a naval base. He worked there with all the means in his power and all his energy. He drove back the sands carried by the waters from the dikes. Thus, behind the glorious victories of the king, Vauban, digger of French soil, as Daniel Halévy calls him in his fine book, fixed the boundaries of his country and established them so strongly that they still remain on the foundations he gave them.

During the war with Holland it was he who seized Maestricht and directed the trench works in person. He then became commander-in-chief of the army. He took Valenciennes and Cambrai and, each time, as soon as the town had fallen, he organized it and put it in a state of defense.

That same year he became general commissary of fortifications. Without any rest or relaxation he scoured France from the Rhine to the Alps, from the Alps to the Pyrenees, from the Pyrenees to Flanders, from Flanders to Brittany. The slightest mound of earth raised for the defense of the territory was his business. He strengthened all existing fortresses and raised new ones: Maubeuge, Longwy, Thionville, Hagueneau, Huningue, Kehl and Landau formed a continuous barrier round the country. He was present everywhere, and everywhere adapted himself to the nature of the soil, rock or waters.

In 1683 it was this barrier of fortified towns that saved the country.

He took Mons, Namur, Steinkerque and finally, in 1703, became a field marshal. This new honor did not drive him away from danger and labor, he even protested against its privileges. He wanted to be able to go again into the trenches, among those trench-digging soldiers who besieged towns. He also arranged not to be far from the fighting line. Under the command of the Duke of Burgundy, it was he who besieged Brisach and who, with the help of the river, took back this town and the fortifications he had himself built.

Any résumé of his career is enough to give an idea of this surprising rhythm of work, battles, concentration and constantly recurring cares. The whole life of Vauban is the indefatigable march of a great captain from one frontier to another, and the simple chronology of his victories speaks for itself. But, in the midst of brilliant military exploits, it is difficult for us to realize the everyday labor and the daily concern of this man for France. Let us listen to him when he speaks for himself at the end of his life:

"I take the liberty of being allowed to speak of myself for the first time in my life. I am now in my seventy-third year, with the burden of fifty-two years of service and fifty important sieges and nearly forty years of continual journeys and visits to frontier towns. All this has been for me the occasion of much trouble and fatigue, both mental and physical, for there has never been for me any summer or winter."

What more could be said, how could it be said better? Behind the man of war, we perceive something great: a man entirely devoted to his country, whose single passion, whose very reason for being, was the service of his country. There is no doubt that Vauban's military fame would suffice to make him great. No doubt that with victories, towns besieged and fallen, fortresses saved from the enemy, Vauban would be ranked with the greatest captains. He used for the first time the ground-level fortifications of modern times. It was he who conceived crossfires, hollow cannon balls, ricochets, elevations of earth; he, too, who perfected parallel trenches and who altered the sap trenches. Finally it was he who gave French infantry the weapon that has triumphed in battles for two centuries: the bayonet and the rifle.

But what we would call today the Great Citizen is even greater in Vauban than the great captain. If for forty years he scoured France in "continual journeys and visits to frontier towns," he learned to know and to love this country. No doubt later experience complemented the first impressions and friendships of his youth. He knew that war is not a goal and that it is only in peace that the foundation of real grandeur of states can be laid. He was worried that "we have fluttered like butterflies beyond the Alps instead of making safe the frontier fortresses." He asked especially that the good of the people be our main concern. Let us listen to him again:

"It seems to me that at all times, the lower class has not been thought of sufficiently in France and that little has been done for it. Thus it is the most ruined and most miserable class of the kingdom. It is this class, however, which is the most numerous and does the country the most real and effective service. . . . It is this class that produces soldiers and sailors . . . and a great number of officers, all the merchants and lesser magistrates. It is this class which practices and fills all crafts and trades; manages all the trade and factories of the kingdom, furnishes all the laborers and wine-growers of the country districts, takes care of the cattle, sows the wheat and harvests it, makes the wine; in a few words, it is this class which does all big and small tasks of country and town."

How could we speak better, at the present time, of this people of France? Vauban was doubtless a loyal servant of king and country, but he wanted the State to serve the people. He was indignant with the profiteers and prevaricators:

"Chance would have it that I should have been born the poorest gentleman in the kingdom, but as a compensation I was given a loyal heart so alien to all sorts of dishonesty that it cannot bear even the thought of it without horror."

These feelings led him to take a part in politics, to see further than his time, further than the duties of his position. This Great Citizen searched his heart and saw clearly the essential duties of any citizen—duties that were contrary to the beliefs of his time. He meditated, conceived, set in order a plan of reform, and as a logical sequence found himself, a century in advance, in conflict with this monarchy whose service had been the reason of his very existence.

If, by his military works, Vauban scales the heights for the French monarchy, with the *Dîme royale*[1] he opens the controversial discussion that will lead the French people to become its own sovereign. Thus in the loyalty of his labor as well as in the rational criticism of the State, Vauban remains faithful to the profound forces of the people of France.

That is why, after three hundred years, the govern-

[1]Projet d'une dîme royale *was the full title of Vauban's book. It advocated the suppression of all existing taxes and the establishment of one to be applied impartially to all classes. Presented to Louis XIV in 1707, the book displeased the king and brought Vauban into disgrace.*

A Great Servant Of The Nation: Vauban
ment of the Republic can commemorate his memory,
since the run of the centuries and the profound muta-
tions of time have failed to antiquate this great servant
of the nation in the minds of the French of today.

*Speech delivered at the celebration of the tercentenary
of Vauban.*